FAMILY WELFARE IN INDIA

A CROSS-CULTURAL STUDY

FAMILY WELFARE IN INDIA
A CROSS-CULTURAL STUDY

By

N.K. Behura

&

R.P. Mohanty

Nabakrushna Choudhury Centre for
Development Studies, Orissa
Bhubaneswar–751 013

DISCOVERY PUBLISHING HOUSE
NEW DELHI-110002

First Published-2005

ISBN 81-7141-920-8

Published by

DISCOVERY PUBLISHING HOUSE

4831/24, Ansari Road, Prahlad Street,
Darya Ganj, New Delhi-110002 (India)
Phone: 23279245 • Fax: 91-11-23253475
E-mail:dphtemp@indiatimes.com

Printed at:

Amit Enterprises, Delhi

FOREWORD

The greatest problem of India has been its huge population size. Ever since it became a sovereign Republic, it has been trying hard to ensure all-round development for its citizens, particularly the poorer and deprived sections. All its efforts to provide food, shelter, housing, basic education, primary health care services, communication, safe drinking water and clean environment are set at naught because of rapid population explosion. By the end of this year, the total population of India is likely to be around 102 crores. If, population of the country continues to increase at such a rapid rate, it will be difficult to meet the basic needs of the people. Further, if the development of the economy does not protect to all the people, the gap between the well-to-do and the hapless downtrodden is bound to increase. This, trend, if continues unabated, will push millions of people to an irredeemable situation of deprivation.

Indian society is pluralistic in its structure with different segments of groups of populations based on language, religion, caste, ethnicity and sect, which create socio-political schism. All the groups have different characteristic features and are different from one another in some way or the other. And further, the impact of modernization is absolutely not uniform on all sections of Indian population. Therefore, lack of education, prevalence of traditionalism and age-old belief pattern militate against small family norm. The son factor is the greatest stumbling block, which precludes adoption of contraceptive devices to limit the family size. The process of procreation continues till a son is born to a married couple.

The present work: "Family Welfare in India: A Cross Cultural Study" was undertaken by Prof. N.K. Behura and Dr. R.P. Mohanty of Anthropology section of the Centre and successfully completed. This, in fact, is the fourth study in the series of current social problems of the study programme.

I thank Professor N.K. Behura and Dr. R.P. Mohanty for the immense trouble they have taken in preparing this important study. Prof. Behura is a source of inspiration to all the social scientists and his effort, dedication and intellectual endeavour deserve commendation. Dr. R.P. Mohanty's sincere and devoted work has made it possible to complete the study in a record time. I thank both of them again for their support and guidance to the centre.

This book will be very useful for the development planners, NGOs activists, academicians, researchers, students, demographers and all those who are interested in the study of population problem in general and Family Welfare in particular.

(Prof. B. Misra)
Former Director and Chairman
and at present Research Advisor,
N.K.C. Centre for Development Studies,
Orissa

PREFACE

Indian population is growing alarmingly because of various interrelated factors. With a view to brake the pace of population growth great emphasis has been giving on family welfare programmes since last few decades. But since India is a very vast country with great cultural and religious diversities and huge differentiation in educational attainment and economic advancement among different communities, uniform family welfare programmes are not so satisfactorily being productive. There are many independent variables that significantly affect the family welfare programmes in rural areas.

Considering this Indian characteristics feature, in this book an attempt has been made to show a comparative picture on family planning and associated factors cross-culturally among four communities belonging to different social strata of the broader Indian social order. The prime thrust of the study concentrates on eight important aspects, such as: (i) Nature of Indian society and rules of residence, (ii) Notion of marriage and attainment of parenthood, (iii) Notion of sex preference in birth, the girl child and family planning, (iv) Attitude of potential couples toward family planning measures, (v) Factors associated with tubectomy vis a vis vasectomy, (vi) Sources of information on family planning measures, (vii) Post operation complications and (viii) Government facilities and level of awareness among the people etc. Apart from all these the book provides a separate chapter on suggestive measures that could be adopted for more success of family welfare programme in a welfare country, like India.

This book will be very useful to various personnel, including the demographers, professional social scientists, researchers, NGOs activists, and all those who are interested in demography in general and family planning in particular.

Authors

CONTENTS

CHAPTER–I

INTRODUCTION

With 16 per cent of the world's population, India ranks as the second most populous country of the world and her population is still growing very fast as compared to other nations. The population size of this country was only about 24 crores (238,396,327) during 1901. It grew upto 36 crores (361,088,090) in 1951 and it had ultimately reached a huge figure of about 85 crores (846,362,688) in the last census year, i.e., 1991. The population experts had projected that the population size of this country would touch 100 crore mark by the end of the century but surprisingly the population is growing so rapidly that it has already crossed this mark much before the completion of the target period. The current projected population as being telecast everyday through the electronic media of television was approaching to be 101 crore by the end of December, 2000. This trend of population growth has undoubtedly created a lot of insurmountable pressure on the available natural resources as the density of population per. sq. kilometre is alarmingly increasing over the periods coinciding with the population growth. It has been increased from 117 in 1901 to as many as 267 in 1991 and there has been no significant achievement in the restoration and upgradation of such resources for maintenance of a balanced ecosystem with the present strength of population and accommodating the future population. This, in other hand stands as a deterrent to the economic as well as social development of the country.

The reasons of such a rapid population growth in India are much which are interrelated and multidimensional in nature. The important reasons may be attributed to various demographic, socio-cultural, religious and economic aspects. We may discuss these aspects here in a nutshell.

So far as the demographic aspects are concerned, high birth rate compared to low death rate cause population growth. The mortality rate is progressively being reduced over the past several decades because of tremendous advancement in medical science and availability of better health care facilities for more and more people year after year. This has also increased the life expectancy of Indian population. Apart from this, immigration of population from other countries to India is also an important factor to this effect. People from different parts of the world come to India as this country is a developing one and there is tremendous scope for earning.

India is a heterogenous country consisting of people of a number of races, languages, religions and cultures spreading from one end of the country to another. Each community has its own ideology, ethics and ways of leading life depending upon its cultural values and religious codes of conduct. Still then some common features are marked among these communities. More than 75 per cent of Indian people reside in rural areas and most of them are educationally backward. Hence they are normally very tradition-bound and their world view and awareness level on various vital aspects of life, like health, family, marriage, pregnancy, obtaining parenthood, limiting family size, rearing of progenies etc. is very limited.

In our country, marriage is considered as a social as well as religious rite without which an individual cannot be considered as a full-fledged person, be it a man or woman. As such a married person can perform certain important rituals for the well being of its family or even for its community members as a whole. However, marriage is not everything for a person to raise the social status and prestige rather becoming a parent after marriage is more essentially required. A couple has to prove its fertility within a certain period of time, otherwise it has to gradually lose its social status and ritual importance in the family as well as in the community depending upon the delay period in conception of the female spouse. Generally in all the Indian religions sterility is considered as a sin and in Orissa a couple that is unable to produce a child after marriage is not tolerated by its family members. Such a couple is referred to as *Banjha,* meaning barren, in a derogatory sense and thus is highly humiliated and ill-treated in society but what is actually more surprising and astonishing is that mere proving of fertility by procreating a single child is not enough. Such a couple is referred to as *Kakabandya*. It is also not free from humiliation, but certainly in such a case the couple is not generally ill-treated either by the family members or by any of the community members. By procreating a single child a couple may prove its fertility and hence can raise its social prestige and ritual importance, but the couples who prove their fertility again and again by procreating a number of progenies are more respectable. Thus, a couple having a number of children feels very proud and exemplify itself for others and even do not forget to compare its successful parenthood with the parenthood of epic and historic characters, like that of Dhrutarashtra and Gandhari of Dwapara epoch, who had as many as hundred sons. On the contrary such epic and historic characters have also greatly influenced and created a craze among the rural people to procreate many children a couple can. In this context the literature of Charaka Samhita explains that "A person with numerous children was considered *mangalya* (auspicious), *prasansaya* (worthy of praise) *viryavana* (virile) and *shakhaukta* (repository/in possession of many branches of families)", (Quoted in Raina, 1990: 42). Moreover, as sterility is considered as a sin, people consider high fertility as a ritual merit and the progenies born to a couple are thus considered as the gift of God and even in our country the infants and children are considered as the icons of the God itself. Therefore, many believe that the number of progenies a couple gets, absolutely depends on the will of the God, and, as a result of this, one must not restrict its family size by adopting mechanical methods of birth-control. If at all one does like this, it may go against the well wishes of the Almighty and hence the couple may face some mishaps.

Moreover, most of the Indian communities are patriarchal, patrilineal and patrilocal in nature. These systems essentially need to have at least one male child per couple in order to inherit and manage the parental properties to perform ritual duties and to look after parents during their old age. If more number of male children are born to a couple than it is well and good as in that case the security of the ancestral properties is highly ensured and the risk of leading life alone during old age is much lessened. But a couple is left to have male or female issues by chance factors as formation of sex of the progenies born to it is absolutely a biological phenomenon and man cannot do anything to alter the sex of a child depending upon its own wish and desire. But as the tradition demands, it has to have a male child for fulfilling the said obligations and obtaining others interests from it. This compels a couple to prefer a male child over a female one and to fulfil this anxiety, the couple goes on procreating children one after one until it gets a male issue. But as the child mortality was very high in our country during the past and as even today to trend in the rate of decline in infant or child mortality is not so satisfactory, most of the parents do not remain satisfied with only one male issue rather they tend to procreate more male children with anticipated future deaths of any one or more of their male children. With this anticipation they produce more children than actually what they want and thus this trend of procreation certainly expedite the process of population growth at the familial level.

Apart from the above factors, in patriarchal societies, male children are considered as economic assets and girls as economic and social burden since the latter are to leave their parental home after their marriage and reside permanently with their husband in their in-laws house. Any major expenditure on bringing up and education of these children is not appreciated by most of the parents and considered as financial loss for the parents. Moreover, the parents are to face a lot of problems for marriage of their daughters that includes arrangement of huge dowry. Therefore even now-a-days women who are unable to give birth to a male child suffer from humiliation and ill-treatment. A recent piece of news published in the Oriya daily 'The Samaj', on 24th July, 2000, points out that "Murali Mehentar of Kumbharmuli village under Bhogarai Police Station, after 16 years of his marital life, is still torturing his wife physically as because she has given birth to five female children but not a single male issue. Even Murali, now prepares for his second marriage with a hope that he would be blessed with a son from his would be second wife Pratima, Muralis first wife has filed a case in the village panchayat and also in the local police station but still she has not yet got any justice. She has also informed the District Magistrate and the Superintendent of Police after she failed to have any result from the local village panchayat and the police station. But still she has not got any result from these high officials. Now she is leading a vary hard and wretched life by selling bamboo baskets to earn her livelihood". The silence of the village committee and the government indicate as if practically Pratima has committed a grave mistake by giving birth to five female children and her husband is really an innocent man. In another event in Bangladesh, a neighbouring patrilocal Muslim nation where Indian culture persists, a man, namely, Abdul Baren, aged 40 of the village Ukiary in Manikganj district has recently cut down the nose of her wife Rahena who had already given birth to four girl children and the fifth one being the same. Abdul was away when the delivery took place but rushed to her wife in anger with a sharp knife and indulged in the case when he came to know the matter (The Samaj, 16.12.2000).

However, as presently the Indian population has exploded to an alarming stage, various economic and social pressure is steadily mounting on parents. They face a lot of difficulties in feeding and educating their children, providing suitable income opportunities, and even providing them with a piece of land for the basic need of constructing a house for residential purpose. Therefore awareness on the benefits of limiting family size through birth control measures is gradually increasing among them. Side by side the government and non-government agencies are playing a major role in motivating the public to limiting the family size with the help of various electronic and other media, like television, radio, newspapers, booklets, pamphlets, pictures, etc.

In India, family planning movement was first started in the year 1949 when the famous lady Rama Rao who was the President of All India Women's Conference in 1946-47, started Family Planning Association of India (Raina, 1990: 104). Prior to the formation of this association, observing the alarming growth trend of Indian Population, Prof. Gopalji Ahluwalia, Prof. of Ramjas College, Delhi, had started an institution on birth control called 'Indian Birth Control Society' in 1922. But it did not last long for some reasons (cf. ibid, p. 89). However, the Family Planning Association of India has been actively working since its inception. But various family planning methods were introduced in different states of the country one by one only after 1952 when Family Planning Programme (FPP) was first launched in 1952. Currently the Indian family planning approach is based on promotion of "responsible parenthood with a two-child family norm (regardless of sex of the children), through the voluntary use of contraceptive methods best suited to each couple and a variety of material and child health schemes" (Ministry of Health and Family Welfare, 1991 as cited in PRC and IIPS, 1993: 9). Presently there are four types of modern family planning methods, like (i) sterilisation, that is vasectomy for the male and tubectomy for the female spouse, (ii) intra-Uterine Device (IUD) insertions, (iii) use of conventional contraceptives and (iv) use of oral pills. Of these, sterilisation is a permanent method of birth control and others are utilised as spacing methods. These family planning methods are being operated "through the existing network of Primary Health Centres (PHCs), Sub-Centres, and Referral Centres called Community Health Centres, and also through Village Health Guides and Traditional Birth Attendants at village level" (PRC and IIPA, 1993: 9). Thus, a couple can get the required information and assistance from various points and persons both in rural as well as in urban areas but the result in adoption of birth control measures among the eligible couples is not found to be satisfactory. The data available in 'Selected Socio-Economic Statistics of India, 1999; reveal that currently there are only 44 per cent of eligible couples (1998-99) who are practising family planning. This, otherwise, signifies that as many as 56 per cent of eligible couples are left without having any family planning. Thus they are more prone to conception and hence procure children. Unless a steadily reverse trend is achieved in near future, India would face more and more economic, social, political and other associated problems in future. But in this country a sudden satisfactory achievement in adoption of birth control measures is not possible. This is because more than 70 per cent of the population of this country reside in rural areas and only about little more than 50 per cent people of the total population are literate and the literacy for women is much lower as compared to the men. Moreover, India is a very vast country having crores of people belonging to a number of varied communities, castes, religions, cultures etc. They are not equally advanced in the sectors of education, economy, health, political participation and awareness, decision making and planning family because of their differential mode of leading life. This is very much conditional to the local geographical and ecological factors. Therefore, as it is very difficult and expensive for a poor country, like India, we do not have specific community and caste-wise data on birth control measures basing on which strategic plans could be formulated, and thus family planning programme could be more successful in this country as compared to other poor and developing nations of the world. Therefore, it is now very essential and important to think in this regard and formulate action plans accordingly.

India is mainly inhabited by the Hindus and the Hindu social organisation is broadly divided into four segments, like Brahman (priestly group), Kshyatriya (militia group), Vaishay (trading group) and Shudra (artisan group or serving castes). The people of these four segments are called as Varna group and the others are called as non-varna or Avarna or as the fifth-born or Panchama. These people are otherwise known as Harijan who are now officially scheduled in the constitution of India and hence termed as the Scheduled Castes. Likewise the Hindu social organisation also does not include the hill and forest dwelling people, who are traditionally known as Girijan or Adivasi. They have also been referred to as sub-human beings or Banamanisa or Aranyaka in various parts of our country. Like the Harijans, the tribal people have also been scheduled in the constitution and hence are termed as the Scheduled Tribes.

The socio-economic background of these three category of people, viz. people belonging to varna order, Scheduled Castes and Scheduled Tribes distinctly differ from one another. Likewise, the economic condition and the educational status also differ from one another to a great extent. Accordingly there is a great disparity in their thinking process and awareness level.

Therefore, in the above context, in the present study, a sincere attempt has been made to analyse the field reality on different aspects concerning to the aspects of family planning among the people of different social category, like Brahman from the upper caste Hindu social order, Chasa from the middle caste Hindu social order and Scheduled Caste and tribal people who are outside the Hindu social organisation. It will provide a comparative cross-cultural picture on the problem of population growth basing on which future visualisation could be made and probable action plan be formulated to tackle the problem.

Aims and Objectives of the Study

Basing on the above problem, the broad aims and objectives of the present study will be to find out

- *(a)* the notion of marriage and obtaining parenthood among the targeted population,
- *(b)* the notion regarding sex preference in birth and importance of son vis-à-vis daughter,
- *(c)* attitude towards family planning and adoption of birth control measures,
- *(d)* adoption of birth control measures among eligible couples,
- *(e)* sources of information about family planning and birth control measures,
- *(f)* reasons of adoption and non-adoption of birth control measures,
- *(g)* post-operation complications,
- *(h)* awareness level as regards government schemes/ facilities on family planning and

(i) to provide a recipe for the better implementation and success of family planning programmes in India.

The Universe and Methodology

The Universe

The universe of the study constitutes a total number 200 eligible couples, with 50 couples each from upper caste Hindu social order, i.e. Brahman or priestly caste, Hindu peasants, i.e. Chasa or agriculturists belonging to the middle caste Hindu social order and ex-untouchables or Scheduled Caste i.e. Bauri or agricultural labourers and Scheduled Tribe, i.e. Santals who are settled in different slums of Bhubaneswar city and hence work as construction workers, rickshaw pullers, vendors, etc.

Sampling Procedure

The study is confined to five heterogeneous caste Hindu villages and two slums. The villages are situated on the outskirts of Bhubaneswar city, the state capital of Orissa and the slums are located within the municipal boundary of the city. All the villages and slums fall in Bhubaneswar block and hence belong to the Khordha district of the state.

The study villages were selected on the basis of purposive random sampling depending upon the presence of the targeted caste groups, like Brahman, Chasa and Bauri. This limitation was imposed on selection of the villages because village institutions composed with these castes are considered as ideal ones where more or less all traditional characteristics of Indian village organisation are evident. However, since the villagers belonging to coastal districts of the state normally do not constitute tribal population and as a part of the objectives of the study to work out the objectified issues cross-culturally, we have selected two slums within the Bhubaneswar city where the tribal people, particularly the Santals are available.

As to the selection of couples, emphasis was laid on the selection of those who are eligible and those who are bio-physically able to produce children. However, importance was given to the age specifications of female spouses as indicated (15-49) by the experts and the government.

Research Design

The whole sample couples have been divided equally (50 each) into different castes and tribes and then intra-community comparison has been made. Similarly, both the male and female spouses of each caste/community have been kept apart to make intra-community comparison on certain specific issues.

Research Tools Used

The study has made use of a specific schedule for recording of data or socio-economic aspects as well as on various issues concerning the objectives of the study. Apart from this, various case studies have been recorded, and group discussions were made with the couples. Due importance has been given to group discussions with the aged couples with a view to know their views and attitude towards family planning. This has been done as the tradition passes from the older generation to the younger ones through lip service and hence the whole heritage is imbibed by the progenies.

Data Processing

The data collected from the primary source were first scrutinized and then transferred to a master sheet manually. Thereafter, specific tables were designed depending upon the aims and objectives of the study. Apart from the primary data, the study has also made use of data collected from secondary sources which were processed manually and presented both in tabular and descriptive forms.

Nature of Study

The nature of the present study is of one-time cross-cultural one since it has intended to focus a comparative picture on different issues concerning family planning practice among different sections of Indian society residing in a common social and physical habitat. At the same time, this is also a cross-sectional study since it has focussed the disparities existing on various issues between male and female spouses of each caste/community studied.

Review of Literature

Indian population problem has reached its peak. Considering the gravity of the problem a number of social science researchers, academicians, demographers, etc. have conducted a number of studies on different aspects of the problem.

Raina (1990) has made a study on family planning tradition in India. He has vividly discussed various aspects of family planning ranging from pre-vedic time to early 1950. In his work he has described different historical aspects, specifically the family planning practices prevailed among different religious communities, like Hindu, Muslim, Christian, Jews and Zorastrians, during pre-vedic and post-vedic periods He has also explored the family planning movement in India very lucidly since the early nineteenth century till around 1950. However, his study mainly analyses the anthropological works, archaeological excavations and vedic literatures including Rigveda, Atharva veda, Upanishadas, Manu Samhita, Kautilya's Arthasastra and Vatsayan's writings. He has also focussed on various important human aspects relating to family planning, sexual behaviour of human beings, forms and evaluation of marriage, desired number of children, role of yoga and medicine for sexual vigour and fertility and herbal ingredients used for abortion and remove infertility. He has also provided some vital field level revelations or rethem method of birth control measures.

Reddy (1997) has worked on the feasibility on the practice of two-child norm among rural people in India. He has taken six sub-urban villages of Chandragiri Taluk surrounding Tirupati district of Andhra Pradesh on the basis of purposive random sampling.

From amongst the sample villages, he has selected 400 eligible couples of which 200 are adopters of family planning devices and the rest 200 couples are non-adopters. He has discussed issues like expectations of additional children, reasons for non-adoption of family planning measures, opinion of future use of family planning among the non-adopters.

He has deduced that only 7 per cent of rural couples are adopting family planning and merely 3 per cent use this who have two living girl children with them. However, significantly very high proportion of the rural couples (31.50%) is adopting family planning measures who have, on an average, 3.62 living children with the sex-ratio of two male and varying number of female children. Moreover, only 3.5 per cent couples have an average number of 6 living children who are adopting family planning measures.

Visaria, Visaria and Jain's (1995) work is on contraceptive use and fertility situation in the state of Gujarat. Their study is based on a comprehensive survey of about 13,600 households covering a total population of 10 million in four districts of the said state. The districts which they have studies are: Bharuch, Panchmahal, Kheda and Rajkot.

The broad objectives of their study were to:

(i) identify the degree of consistency between the estimate of contraceptive prevalence rate based on the survey (contraceptive prevalence rate) and the estimate of couple protection rate based on service statistics;

(ii) identify the source of inconsistency between the district-level estimates of contraceptive use based on service statistics and surveys;

(iii) identify the relationship between reported contraceptive prevaler ce rate and fertility, and

(iv) identify the programme and non-programme factors that may be responsible for the district-level differentials in contraceptive prevalence rate.

The findings of the study shows that the service statistics relating to the acceptors of IUDs, condoms and pills overstate the use of reversible methods.

They conclude that in Gujarat (Bharuch, Kheda and Rajkot) fertility has declined by at least 50 per cent since the early 1960s.

A national survey on 'Family Welfare' was made in different states of India during 1992-93. In Orissa, this survey was conducted between 7th March, 1993 and 18th June, 1993 by Population Research Centre, Bhubaneswar and International Institute for Population Sciences, Bombay. The survey result is based on 4257 ever-married women falling in the age group of 13-49. The sample of ever-married women was lifted from 4602 households.

This survey has brought out several amazing information on various vital aspects like, current marital status, age at first marriage, age at first co-habitation, marriage between relatives, fertility, family planning, morbidity and mortality, maternal and child health, infant feeding and child nutrition etc. The findings of the study have been shown in respect of the whole state under the broad category of rural and urban break-up.

Ramu (1988) has conducted a very significant study on the trend of fertility pattern in relation to family structure among different religious groups, like Hindu, Muslim and Christians in Kolar Gold Field of Karnataka state. He had set five objectives which are: (i) to explore the nature of marriage and family in an urban Indian context, (ii) to explore the prepared family size and valuation of children by parents in relation to their marital and family patterns, (iii) to examine how fertility decisions are made, (iv) to analyse the attitude towards and practice of fertility regulation among the respondents, and (v) to delineate how changing perceptions of marriage, family and family size affect the decisions of couples on fertility.

He finds that most of the couples irrespective of religion perceive large family as a source of potential strain for themselves and also for their children. He concludes that fertility decisions are made not only in relation to the couples own marital and familial appreciations but with regard to the social environment in which the children are brought up. The aspects which create a negative impact on the parents to have large family size, are the scarcity in goods and services, limited opportunities for good education and employment. He also points out that dowry dominated market has also created a great impact on them to reduce the family size. Finally he says that the considerations influencing the number of children desired are changing and this will eventually have an impact on population growth of our country.

In a study, Shariff (1989) focuses on various socio-economic correlates of the fertility decline in different rural areas of South India. He has concentrated his work in villages, like Ramagere, Laxmipura, Shivadurga and Gowdahall and Castes like Brahman, (Priest), Lingayat (Agriculturist), Balagiga (Bangle dealer), Ediga (Toddy tappers), Kuruba (Shepherds), Golla (Shepherds), Ganiga (Oil Crusher), Madivala (Washerman), Achari (Smiths), Nayarda (Barber), Bovi (Stone cutters), Petty (Traders), etc. He has explored various aspects of differential fertility, effects of changing family structure, and intra-family relationship on fertility and pattern of fertility decision-making.

He finds that in villages, like Ramagere, voluntary acceptance of family planning started from castes, like Brahman, Bidigas and Balagigas who had greater access to urban areas and hence contact with the urban people. The castes like Kurubas, Gollas, various service castes and Scheduled Caste and also the Muslims did not accept the IUDs because of imperfect and poor knowledge about the devices. Adoption of family planning through tubectomy is very rare since this is a permanent method of family planning and the people normally do not favour undergoing tubectomy who do not have at least three children, two sons and one daughter.

He concludes that the women have created a positive impact on the men because of their higher level of awareness and participation in decision-making in relation to family planning. This has certainly created a noteworthy decline in fertility in the study area. However, he observes that this, pattern of change has occurred more frequently in heterogeneous villages as compared to small and remote villages.

Abusaleh (1989) has also conducted a similar study among different castes, like Brahman, Gosian, Jat, Thakur, Baniya, Kayastha, Khatri, Arora, Nai, Dhobi, Gujjar, Darzi, Zhimmer, Khati, Lohar, Chamar, Dhanka, Balmik, etc. residing in Bhiwani city which is situated about 48 kilometer away from Rohtak district of the state of Haryana. He has divided these castes into 3 groups as upper, middle and lower and has tried to explain the relationship between the explanatory variables and fertility with the help of proximate variables, like inter-spouse communication, caste-consciousness country conformity, exposure to printed media contraception etc.

He concludes that family is related to fertility pattern and the fertility is directly related to preponderance of sons over daughters.

Significance, Scope and Limitations of the Study

From the review of the above literature it is found that considering the population problem as a burning issue in our country, many researchers belonging to different disciplines, like demography, sociology, economics, and allied subjects have done a number of studies in the area of population control in different parts of the country. But anthropological and cross-cultural studies on this issue are very limited. Cross-cultural studies are considered as very important in social science research since such studies throw a comparative picture by which a very clear and comprehensive picture on the field situation comes out into the fore and thus planning becomes very easier. But unfortunately no significant micro cross-cultural study on population control has yet been conducted with anthropological perspective with particular reference to the Brahman, Chasa, Bauri and Santal who represent important social sections of broader Indian society in Orissa. Therefore, considering the importance of such a study, we have conducted this study and for these reasons, this study seems to be very significant. But the scope of the study is not so broad since it constitutes a small size of simple population. However, the study would be very useful to the academicians, researchers, development action planners, administrators, NGOs and social activists and to those who are interested on studies concerning population problems, birth control measures, and economic development of the country. The study will provide various theoretical clues for future study. It will also necessitate the researchers to undertake macro studies on this topic by which the scope of this study would be further enhanced.

CHAPTER–II

POPULATION PROFILE AND THE TREND OF FAMILY PLANNING IN INDIA AND ORISSA

Population Trend in India and Orissa

The pace of growth of population in India has caught the attention of the whole world since the percentage of decadal variation in population growth of this developing country is being increased by more than 20 per cent in each census decade after independence. The population of this country, as mentioned in the introductory chapter, was only 238.4 million in 1901. It increased to 252.1 million in 1911. This indicates a growth of about 1.4 crore of population which is (+) 5.75 per cent of the total population of 1901. This otherwise means that during the first census decade the percentage of decadal population variation was only (+) 5.75. This percentage variation in population growth, went on increasing steadily from one decade to another and it reached to 361.1 million in 1951 showing 13.31 per cent of decadal variation over the population of the preceding census year i.e. 1941. However, the population growth has more or less remained within 13.31 per cent per decade in between 1911 and 1951. The critical period for India started from the decade of 1951-61, that is, after independence as the growth rate unexpectedly jumped from (+) 13.31 to + 21.51 during this decade. It further increased to 24.80 per cent in the next succeeding decade, i.e. 1961-71. It was however, reduced to + 24.66 per cent in the decade of 1971-81 and (+) 23.85 per cent in the last census decade, that is, 1981-91. In an aggregate the Indian population has so far increased by (+) 254.48 per cent in between 1901 and 1991 (Table 2.1).

This type of population growth is certainly not favourable for a developing nation, like India. It is definitely becoming a lethal and marauder to the Indian economy and hence it stands as a deterrent for a wholesome development of the country. However, the trend of population growth in Orissa is also more or less similar to that of the national scenario. But it has some specific and striking features. In the first census decade the population of this state had grown by (+) 10.14 per cent as compared to only (+) 5.75 of India. But the trend was reversed in the decade of 1941-51, while this figure was 13.31 per cent for India for the said decade, it was only (+) 6.38 for Orissa.

In the decade of 1961-71, Orissa had witnessed a growth of 25.05 per cent as the highest percentage of population growth ever found in any decade in the scenario of Indian population growth. However, there was a declining trend in population growth of India in the decade of 1971-81 and 1981-91 compared to the decade of 1961-71, Orissa also shows a similar trend but while the percentage of decadal variation of Indian population got reduced from 24.66 in 1971-81 to 23.85 in 1981-91, in case of Orissa it was reduced to 20.17 in the 1971-81 decade and to 20.16 during 1981-91. However, the population growth rate of both India as well as Orissa seems to be very high.

From 1901 to the latest census year, i.e. 1991, it was only during the census year of 1921 the population size of both India as well as Orissa was reduced in comparison with the population of the previous census year. In this year, the Indian population was short by 772,177 as against 220,289 of Orissa. This indicates a negative decadal variation by 0.31 percentage point for India and 1.94 for Orissa. This negative trend did not occur for the reason that the people become more conscious of the burden of large family size and thus practised family planning measures through adoption of family planning measures. Rather, it so happened because of the great famine that had taken a heavy toll of human life, during this period.

Density of Population

Density of population means the average number of people living in one square kilometre of surface area. According to the statistics available in 1951 census, the density of Indian population was 117 persons per sq. kilometre which increased to 142 in 1961, 177 in 1971, 216 in 1981, and 267 in 1991. For the State of Orissa, these figures are 94 in 1951, 113 in 1961, 141 in 1971, 169 in 1981 and 203 in 1991 census (Table 2.3).

As the increased in density of human population has a direct bearing on the population growth, it is obvious that coinciding with the population growth, density of population would also increase, which is quite natural. But what is actually a problem for us is that we procreate progenies as per our own volition, while we are not able to increase the amount of productive land proportionate to the need of the population. The area of earth is naturally constant and we, the human beings cannot do anything to bring any physical change in the size of the universe. Therefore, people of different nations share it as per the human laws formulated at international levels. Therefore, as mentioned above, picture of land and its ratio to population are steadily becoming grimmer from decade to decade, it creates a heavy pressure on natural resources available in India and Orissa. In urban areas, the density of population is becoming more and more acute year by year, and for this, we face multifaceted problems which have, no doubt, created heavy psychological, physical, economic, social and cultural pressure on all of us. This is, of course unprecedently reducing our quality of life so far as the utilisation of natural resources is concerned. From the economic point of view, density of population increases when economic development occurs but certainly reduction or persistence of same density of population does not mean low economic development or stagnant economy as economic development could be possible with unsteady population growth which is possible through creation of small families by the way of birth control measures. This could leave people in a balanced eco-system and scientific plan and programmes are to be made in this context.

Sex Ratio in India and Orissa

Sex ratio is normally understood as the proportion of females to males. Statistically the proportion is understood as the number of females to 1000 males.

There has never been parity in sex ratio in Indian population. As a result of this, it is considered as an important aspect in Indian population studies. The disparity is observed because, in this tradition-bound country both the male and female sexes have their respective social, cultural, ritual and economic significance and importance in the society.

As observed from the data available in Table No. 2.4, India does not possess a favourable sex ratio as the men have always outnumbered the females and hence there has never been an equal proportion between the sexes. But what is more important to observe from the census data is that excepting the census year of 1981, the proportion of females to males has been steadily decreasing from one census year to another beginning from the first census year (1901) to the latest census conducted in 1991. The sex ratio was 972 in 1901, which was gradually reduced to 930 in 1971. In 1981, it was however, increased to 934 but again it fell to 927 in 1991 (Table 2.4).

Contrary to the above trend, in Orissa, the females have always outnumbered the males in all the decades until 1951. But in 1951, Orissa had, however, a favourable sex ratio, which was 1001. In the next succeeding census years it was 988 in 1971, 981 and 1981 and 971 in 1991. Thus, in the state, the sex ratio has also started falling down since 1971 onwards and as mentioned above, now there are only 971 females per 1000 males in Orissa.

The reasons for the declining sex ratio in India, as mentioned above, may be attributed to various socio-cultural, demographic, ritual and economic factors but no concrete explanation could be made against this. In Indian society, there is preponderance of males over females because of the prevailing system of patriarchy, patrilineage and patrilocality for which female birth is not generally welcome by majority of people.

Moreover, the rate of malnutrition and infant mortality is more among the females as they are given second priority on feeding compared to the male children. For male preference, females are subjected to maternal mortality relating to pregnancy, child birth, poor child care [(it was 0.9% in 1992, 1.1% in 1993, 0.9% in 1994 and 1995, and 0.7% in 1996 (GoI. 1999: 40)] female foeticide and infanticide, and "higher fertility and higher mortality levels for females in all the age groups upto 45" (GoI. 2000: 35). Another important reason for the prevalence of unequal sex ratio in Indian population may be due to the fact that more number of males are born as compared to the female births (Table 2.5).

Profile of Population in Vital Reproductive Age Groups and Age at Marriage

A female child normally gets matured at the age of 12-13 in Indian climate. But she becomes able to procreate progenies at a later age (it is 18 as per the present official norms) only when her reproductive organs are fully grown and developed. However, in our country women give birth to children beginning from the age of 15 which is conditional to various socio-cultural and religious factors and limitations, and she retains the ability to procreate successfully until the age of 49. Within this very broad age group of 15-49, we have nearly 50 per cent women of the total women of the country. Such women comprised 49.1 per cent in 1951 as against 47.1 in 1961, 46.0 in 1971, 47.7 in 1981, 50.3 in 1990 and 50.5 in 1994 (Table 2.6). Availability of such a high percentage of women in this broad and vital age group tend to increase the population at a faster rate. Moreover, the strange practice of child marriage system that existed for quite a long period of time in many communities of Indian society, was also a demoralizing factor for us. By this tradition immatured girls had to marry immautured boys but martial conjugation and bearing of legitimate children were allowed only after the brides attained maturity. Because attaining puberty by passing through the first menstrual cycle was widely considered as the most important criterion for allowing a bride to become a mother. This obnoxious practice of marriage at a younger age had, no doubt, been a very crucial factor for high and speeding growth of Indian population. Considering this aspect as well as other allied factors concerning infant and maternal mortality, malnutrition, etc. Government of India passed the Child Marriage Restraint Act in the year of 1971. Subsequently, the minimum age for marriage of a girl was fixed at 18 through the Child Marriage Restraint (Amendment) Act introduced in 1976. Still then the practice of Child Marriage has not yet been eradicated from the Indian society. In this context a very recent news that is published on 15.12.2000, in a leading Oriya daily newspaper, 'The Samaj', may be referred to. It indicates that child marriage is still going on in certain parts of our country freely.

However, the available statistical data also substantiate the practice of child marriage during different periods of time. In this context one may refer to the data relating to the mean age at first marriage of females. It was merely "13.3" (Ahuja, 1992: 51) during the first census decade, i.e. 1901-1911. However, it increased to 15.4 in 1951, 16.1 and 17.1 in 1971. Further it increased to 17.9 in 1981, but even if the minimum age for girls has been kept at 18 years of age through the introduction of Child Marriage Restraint (Amendment) Act, 1976, there has been no much impact. However, after the lapse of about 26 years since the introduction of the aforesaid act, the figure has come to be 19.4 in 1994. Thus by 2000 A.D. the mean age at marriage of girls has increased by about 1.5 years, over 18 years which has been as the minimum age for marriage of a girl.

As the population problem of India is becoming very acute day by day, it seems to be very common for rural girls to get married at such an early age.

Age Specific Fertility Rates and Current Practice of Family Planning in India and Orissa

Age specific fertility rates for different years are mentioned in Table No. 2.8 by rural and urban break-up and by different vital reproductive age groups. This table indicates that in India, the fertility rate is very high in the age group of 20-24 since in this age group it was 250.8 in 1971, 249.5 in 1976, 246.9 in 1981, 252.3 in 1986, 234.0 in 1991 and 238.4 in 1995 thereby indicating more than 200 fertility rate in each of the above years. Similarly, the next succeeding age group, i.e. 25-29 also seems to be an important reproductive age group as in this age group the above trend was maintained upto 1986 and the rate was little below 200 during 1991 and 1995. So far as the first reproductive age group, i.e. 15-19 is concerned, which is found to be an important age group as in this age group the fertility rate was more than 100 in 1971 followed by 83 in 1976, 90.4 in 1981, 91.1 in 1986, 76.1 in 1991 and 55.2 in 1951. In the last reproductive age group which is 45.49, the fertility rates were 24.4, 15.7, 19.6, 14.6, 12.1 and 10.3 in the years of 1971, 1976, 1981, 1986, 1991 and 1995 respectively.

An important revelation which comes into the fore from the data available in the said table is that the fertility rate is more in rural areas than in urban areas in all the reproductive age groups. However, it is a satisfactory trend that the fertility rate is more or less falling down in all the said age groups since 1971 to 1995.

The age specific fertility rate for the State of Orissa is available in the Table No. 2.9. Like the above revelation, it also indicates that both the age groups that is, 20-24 years and 25-29 years are important ones, since, for the first age group of 20-24, the fertility rate was 258.6 in 1982 and it was 264.4 for the age group of 25-29 in 1983. The trend was also more or less same for the year 1983. Like the trend of fertility in India, in Orissa the fertility rate is more in rural areas compared to urban areas in all the reproductive age groups.

Current Practice of Family Planning in India and Orissa

(a) Percentage of Couples Currently Protected in India by Various Methods of Family Planning

Modern family planning methods are mainly of four types, viz., Sterilisation (vesectomy for males and tubectomy for females), Intra-Uterine Devices, (IUD), Oral Pills and Conventional Contraceptives. Sterilisation is a permanent method of family planning and as data show, in India this method is more popular and hence is accepted by more couples compared to other available methods. The couples who are currently and effectively protected under this method account for 20.1 per cent in 1980-

81 as compared to 30.3 per cent in 1990-91, and 29.6 per cent in 1996-97. The couples who are currently protected due to IUD constitute 1.1 per cent of the total eligible couples in 1980-81, 7.0 per cent in 1990-91, and 7.8 per cent in 1996-97. But the couples who are currently protected due to other methods of family planning, like using of oral pills and conventional contraceptives, are comparatively more in number to the total number of couples currently protected due to IUD during the years mentioned above. Their percentages were 3.3 in 1980-81, 12.3 in 1990-91 and 13.5 in 1996-97. Thus, the percentage of both types of couples who are currently using IUD and other methods, like oral pills and conventional contraceptives are gradually increasing from year to year. This trend is not marked among the couples who are currently and effectively protected due to sterilisation as the letters have grown from 20.1 percentage point in 1980-81 to 30.3 percentage point in 1993-94 and then started falling down by reaching 29.6 percentage point in 1996-97. However, if one looks at the figures concerning to the couples currently protected due to all methods, it is found that in 1980-81, 24.4 per cent couples were protected by all methods. After the lapse of five years this figure came to 38.7 per cent and again after 5 years it rose to 49.6 per cent in 1990-91. This pace went on increasing until 1994-95 when more than 52 (52.2) per cent couples came to be protected. But during 1996-97 it has come down to 51.0 per cent. (Table 2.10)

(b) *Percentage of Couples Effectively Protected in Orissa by Various Methods of Family Planning*

Contrary to the facts mentioned above, the couples who are effectively protected show a different picture since there is a technical difference between the couples who are currently protected and the couples who are effectively protected. The couples who are currently protected may discontinue the use of family planning method that they have adopted and thus may go for procreating children after due spacing. These couples always outnumber the couples who are effectively protected by different family planning methods. However, since sterilization is a permanent method of family planning, the couples who have adopted it do not have any scope to discontinue adoption of such method as per their own choice. Hence the couples adopting sterilization are always effective and because of this, the statistical figures remain constant for either group of couples, viz., the couples who are currently protected and also those who are effectively protected under this method. This method is always effective with very meagre chance of failure.

The figures available in Table No. 2.11 indicate that the percentage of couples who are effectively protected due to use of oral pills is less in all the years from 1970-71 to 1996-97 as compared to the couples who are effectively protected by the use of IUD and also those who are protected under the conventional contraceptives. But the percentage of all these three category of couples who are effectively protected by the use of IUD, oral pills and conventional contraceptives are gradually increasing from one year to another. The percentage of couples who are effectively protected by the use of IUD was 1.4 as against 1 per cent of couples using and effectively protected under the conventional contraceptives in 1970-71. These figures increased to 7.4 per cent in case of the former as against 5.2 per cent of the latter in 1996-97. The percentage of couples effectively protected by the use of oral pills was only 0.1 in 1980-81 and it increased to 3.1 per cent in 1996-97.

The couples who are effectively protected by all methods accounted for 10.4 per cent in 1970-71. This figures steadily increased to 45.8 per cent in 1994-95 and then it has started declining, it is 46.5 per cent in 1995-96 and 45.4 per cent in 1996-97 (Table 2.11).

In this background the achievement in the domain of family planning programmes in Orissa is presented in Table No. 2.12. This table indicates that the couples effectively protected in Orissa during 1970-71 through sterilization was 45.43 per cent as compared to 64.93 per cent during 1975-76, 63.96 per cent during 1981-82, 42.94 per cent during 1985-86, 23.35 per cent during 1990-91 and only 19.48 per cent during 1993-94. Thus the couples protected through sterilization is found to be gradually declining over the years in Orissa. But the couples protected by conventional contraceptives are found to show a reverse trend as the percentage of couples protected under this, increased from 27.15 to 34.95 in 1985-86, 49.62 in 1990-91 and finally it has reached to 56.04 in 1993-94. Contrary to this, the couples protected under IUD show a zigzag trend of 27.41 per cent achievement in 1970-71 to 12.45 in 1975-76, 11.88 in 1980-81, 22.11 in 1985-86, 27.02 in 1990-91 and 24.45 in 1993-94. Thus as compared to the protection of couples under sterilization and IUD methods, protection through conventional contraceptives seems to be more successful in Orissa (Table 2.12).

So far as the effective couple protection rate (CPR) through all methods is concerned, Orissa shows a lower rate as compared to the rate of India in all the years beginning from 1990 to 1999. But this rate is higher than the rate of India in the year 1980 and 1985. However, for India this rate is 22.7 in 1980 which increased to 48.6 in 1999 as against 26.9 of Orissa during 1980 and 41.9 during 1999 (Table 2.13). Thus in both the cases, the effective couple protection rate is found to be increasing very steadily but the increase is not so satisfactory.

(c) *Sex-wise Profile of Sterilization*

Sterilization is the safest and permanent method of family planning. It is almost 100 per cent effective in all the cases. Both male and female can be sterilized but only one spouse of a couple is required to be sterilised and by this the couple becomes effective to stop procreation of offsprings. But surprisingly the difference between the percentage of female sterilization (tubectomy) and male sterilization (vesectomy) is very high. As the data show the percentage of tubectomy to the total sterilisation done in different years, is found to be as high as 78.6 in 1980-81 which has steadily increased to 98.1 in 1996-97. There is not a single year in which this percentage has been less than the percentage of previous year. Moreover, there is not a single year in which the percentage of vasectomy has exceeded the percentage of the total cases of tubectomy in India (Table 2.14). The basic reasons for this are many. The main reason is that India is a male dominated society and majority of Indian people reside in rural areas. They are educationally very backward and hence their awareness level is also very low. They have a wrong conception that undergoing sterilization means losing of vigour and vitality that may severely hamper the economy of the family. Most of the Indian communities are patrilineal in which men constitute the main economic resource for the whole family. In that case women do not like to invite any complicacy by forcing their spouses for undergoing sterilization. Moreover, as at the same time such societies are also patriarchal in nature, men influence their spouses to be sterilized and hence keep them in the safe side.

Table—2.1: Decadal variation in population of India (1901-1991)

Census years	*Persons*	*Decadal variation*	*Percentage of decadal variation*
(1)	*(2)*	*(3)*	*(4)*
1901	238,396,327	–	–
1911	252,093,390	(+) 13,697,063	(+) 5.75
1921	251,321,213	(+) 772,177	(-) 0.31
1931	278,977,238	(+) 27,656,025	(+) 11.00
1941	318,660,580	(+) 39,683,342	(+) 14.22
1951	361,088,090	(+) 42,420,485	(+) 13.31
1961	439,234,771	(+) 77,682,873	(+) 21.51
1971	548,159,652	(+) 108,924,881	(+) 24.80
1981	683,329,097	(+) 135,169,445	(+) 24.66
1991	846,302,688	(+) 162,973,591	(+) 23.85
1901-91	–	–	(+) 254.48

Source: General population tables, part-II A (I), Census of India 1991, pp. 314, 322 and 326.

Note: Figures include Jammu and Kashmir.

Table—2.2: Decadal variation in population of Orissa (1901-1991)

Census years	*Persons*	*Decadal variation*	*Percentage of decadal variation*
(1)	*(2)*	*(3)*	*(4)*
1901	10,302,917	–	–
1911	11,378,875	(+) 1,075,958	(+) 10.44
1921	11,158,586	(+) 220,289	(-) 1.94
1931	12,491,056	(+) 1,332,470	(+) 11.94
1941	13,767,988	(+) 1,276,932	(+) 10.22
1951	14,645,946	(+) 877,958	(+) 6.38
1961	17,548,846	(+) 2,902,900	(+) 19.82
1971	21,944,615	(+) 4,395,769	(+) 25.05
1981	26,370,271	(+) 4,425,656	(+) 20.17
1991	31,659,736	(+) 5,289,465	(+) 20.06
1901-91	–	–	–

Source: General population tables, Part-II A, Census of India, 1991, pp. 396-398 and 400.

Table—2.3: Density of population in India and Orissa (1951-1991)

Census years	*India*	*Orissa*
(1)	*(2)*	*(3)*
1951	117	94
1961	142	113
1971	177	141
1981	216	169
1991	267	203

Source: Office of the Registrar General, India as published in selected Socio-Economic Statistics, India, 1999, Govt. of India.

Table—2.4: Sex ratio in India and Orissa (Females per 1000 males)

Census years	India			Orissa
	Rural	Urban	Combined	
1901	979	910	972	1037
1911	975	872	964	1056
1921	970	846	955	1086
1931	966	838	950	1067
1941	965	831	945	1053
1951	965	860	946	1022
1961	963	845	941	1001
1971	949	858	930	988
1981	951	879	934	981
1991	938	894	927	971

Source: General population tables, part-II A (i), Census of India, 1991, pp. 314, 322 and 326, 398 and 400 and selected Socio-Economic Statistics, India, 1999, p. 18.

Note: Figures for india include Jammu and Kashmir.

Table—2.5: Sex ratio at birth (India)

Period	Sex ratio (Males/100 females)
1981-83	109
82-84	110
83-85	110
84-86	110
85-87	110
86-88	110
87-89	110
88-90	110
90-92	111
91-93	112

Source: Women and Men in India, 1998, Central Statistical Organisation, Dept. of Statistics and Programme Implementation, Ministry of Planning and Programme Implementation, Govt. of India, New Delhi p. 4.

Table—2.6: Percentage distribution of population in vital reproductive age groups in India (1951-1994)

Period	0-14		15-49		50+	
	M	F	M	F	M	F
(1)	(2)	(3)	(4)	(5)	(6)	(7)
1951	38.2	38.6	49.7	49.1	12.1	12.2
1961	40.9	41.1	47.2	47.1	11.8	11.7
1971	41.7	42.2	45.8	46.0	12.3	11.8
1981	39.6	39.8	47.7	47.7	12.7	12.5
1990	37.1	36.6	50.4	50.3	12.5	13.1
1994	36.8	36.1	50.4	50.5	12.9	13.5

Source: Family Welfare Programme in India Year Book, 1996-97, GoI, Dept. of FW, Ministry of Health and FW, New Delhi.

Table—2.7: Mean age at marriage (India)

Years	Female	Male
(1)	(2)	(3)
1951	15.4	19.9
1961	16.1	22.3
1971	17.1	22.7
1981	17.9	23.3
1992	19.5	–
1993	19.6	–
1994	19.4	–

Source: Women and Men—India, 1998, GoI.

Table—2.8: Age specific fertility rate in India (1971-1995)

Age groups	*Area*	*Years*					
		1971	*1976*	*1981*	*1986*	*1991*	*1995*
(1)	*(2)*	*(3)*	*(4)*	*(5)*	*(6)*	*(7)*	*(8)*
	Rural	110.6	87.0	98.2	100.3	84.5	61.9
15-19	Urban	64.9	64.6	58.1	62.1	46.1	34.4
	Combined	100.8	83.0	90.4	91.1	76.1	55.2
	Rural	260.9	260.2	261.3	264.6	244.6	256.3
20-24	Urban	213.9	213.7	195.0	217.8	200.7	186.9
	Combined	250.8	249.5	246.9	252.8	234.0	238.4
	Rural	261.6	250.8	244.9	229.4	202.3	203.5
25-29	Urban	227.9	197.5	187.1	179.0	158.7	164.1
	Combined	254.8	238.8	232.1	216.4	191.3	194.2
	Rural	212.4	190.9	180.4	153.6	128.6	134.5
30-34	Urban	158.0	133.9	117.8	94.5	81.6	76.6
	Combined	202.2	179.7	167.7	139.2	117.0	119.1
	Rural	147.5	126.3	112.6	89.3	75.9	67.4
35-39	Urban	96.5	73.6	60.1	45.0	37.4	32.6
	Combined	137.8	116.1	102.5	78.6	66.8	59.2
	Rural	68.2	58.9	48.4	43.5	35.3	37.5
40-44	Urban	34.9	28.9	24.5	17.6	14.9	13.2
	Combined	62.2	53.3	44.0	37.9	30.6	31.0
	Rural	26.3	17.3	22.0	17.8	14.0	12.1
45-49	Urban	15.4	8.3	9.1	4.7	5.3	3.9
	Combined	24.4	15.7	19.6	14.9	12.1	10.3
Total	Rural	5.4	5.0	4.8	4.5	3.9	3.9
fertility	Urban	4.1	3.6	3.3	3.1	2.7	2.6
rate	Combined	5.2	4.7	4.5	4.2	3.6	3.5

Source: **Selected Socio-Economic Statistics, 1998, Central Statistical Organisation, GoI, pp. 30-31.**

***Excludes Jammu and Kashmir.**

Table—2.9: Age specific fertility rate in Orissa (1982-1983)

Age groups	1982			1983		
(1)	(2)	(3)	(4)	(5)	(6)	(7)
15-19	91.7	69.6	89.9	92.6	67.2	90.3
20-24	259.4	150.1	258.6	263.5	272.3	264.4
25-29	232.8	128.1	232.2	252.7	200.9	546.6
30-34	154.3	128.9	151.8	157.3	120.3	153.8
35-39	87.0	60.5	84.4	90.0	55.3	86.7
40-44	33.1	22.7	32.4	39.2	23.8	38.0
45-49	14.1	9.5	13.8	16.7	9.3	16.2

Source: Year book, 1986, Ministry of Health and Family Welfare, GoI as published in Situation Analysis of Women and Children in Orissa, 1991, ORG, Bhubaneswar for UNICEF.

Table—2.10: Percentage of eligible couples currently protected in India by various methods of family planning (1980-81 to 1996-97)

Year	Eligible couples (estimated) in 000	Couples currently & effectively protected due to sterilization	Couples currently protected due to IUD	Couples currently protected due to other methods	Couples currentnly protected due to all methods
(1)	(2)	(3)	(4)	(5)	(6)
1980-81	100.00 (116033)	20.1 (23321)	1.1 (1235)	3.3 (3809)	24.4 (28365)
1985-86	100.00 (129432)	26.5 (34312)	3.9 (5053)	8.3 (10744)	38.7 (50109)
1990-91	100.00 (145140)	30.3 (43947)	7.0 (10173)	12.3 (17814)	49.6 (71933)
1991-92	100.00 (148430)	30.3 (44935)	6.7 (9913)	11.6 (17240)	48.6 (72088)
1992-93	100.00 (151720)	30.3 (45912)	6.6 (100333)	11.9 (18003)	48.7 (73948)
1993-94	100.00 (155020)	30.3 (46964)	7.2 (11108)	13.9 (21489)	51.3 (79561)

(Contd...)

(1)	(2)	(3)	(4)	(5)	(6)
1994-95	100.00 (158310)	30.2 (47771)	7.6 (12003)	13.9 (21963)	51.6 (81737)
1995-96	100.00 (161593)	30.2 (48753)	8.2 (13239)	13.9 (22376)	52.2 (84368)
1996-97	100.00 (164749)	29.6 (48772)	7.8 (12897)	13.5 (22277)	51.0 (83946)

Source: Year Book on Family Welfare Programme in India, 1996-97, Dept. of Family Welfare, Ministry of Health and Family Welfare, GoI, New Delhi, p. 136.

Note: (i) The estimates of couples protected given in the above table are based on (a) age distribution of the acceptors and (b) estimates of joined survivance ratio of husbands and wives in different age groups. Annual attrition rate for IUD acceptors is taken as 37.6% and average annual attrition rate for vasectomy and tubectomy acceptors are taken as follows:

Methods/ period	*1st five year*	*2nd five year*	*3rd five year*	*4th five year*	*5th five year*
Vasectomy	4.11%	7.14%	13.04%	18.74%	33.50%
Tubectomy	2.72%	6.20%	13.52%	28.65%	53.89%

(ii) Figures in brackets represent absolute figures.

Table—2.11: Percentage of eligible couples effectively protected in India and Orissa by various methods of family planning (1970-71 to 1996-97)

Year	*Eligible couples (Estimated) ('000)*	*Couples currently & effectively protected due to sterilization*	*Couples effectively protected due to IUD*	*Couples currently protected due to other methods*		*Couples effectively protected due to all methods*
				Oral pill	*CC users*	
1970-71	94489	8.0	1.4	–	1.0	10.4
1975-76	105239	14.2	1.1	–	1.7	17.0
1980-81	116033	20.1	1.0	0.1	1.6	22.8
1985-86	129432	26.5	3.7	1.1	3.6	34.9
1986-87	132572	27.9	4.5	1.4	3.7	37.5

(Contd...)

1	2	3	4	5	6	7
1987-88	135710	29.0	5.2	1.5	4.2	39.9
1988-89	138850	29.8	5.9	1.7	4.5	41.9
1989-90	141990	30.1	6.3	1.9	5.0	43.3
1990-91	145140	30.3	6.7	2.1	5.1	44.1
1991-92	148430	30.3	6.3	2.2	4.7	43.6
1992-93	151720	30.3	6.3	2.0	4.9	43.5
1993-94	155020	30.3	6.8	2.7	5.6	45.4
1994-95	158310	30.2	7.2	3.0	5.4	45.8
1995-96	161593	30.2	7.8	3.2	5.3	46.5
1996-97	164749	29.6	7.4	3.1	5.2	45.4

Source: **Women and Men in India, 1998 p. 23, Central Statistical Organisation, Dept. of Statistics and Programme Implementation, Ministry of Planning and Programme Implementation, GoI, New Delhi.**

Table—2.12: Achievement of family welfare programmes in Orissa

Year	*Total No. of family welfare centres*	*No. of sterilization done (both vasectomy & tubectomy)*	*No. of IUD*	*No. of C.C. users*	*Total (all methods)*
1970-71	346	97267	58675	58127	214069
1971-72	356	86714	52618	92697	232029
1972-73	356	91859	40964	70869	203692
1973-74	454	55752	28341	39397	123490
1974-75	348	68971	20176	33278	122425
1975-76	331	125040	23976	43558	192574
1976-77	333	322984	19066	42149	384199
1977-78	333	81827	16385	37271	129483
1978-79	333	105058	13945	53520	172523
1979-80	331	90678	17450	47001	155129
1980-81	340	92989	17268	35130	145387
1981-82	340	110130	21089	54255	185474
1982-83	342	146693	30595	85714	263002
1983-84	342	178243	43876	121686	343805
1984-85	345	136376	69742	126090	332208

(Contd...)

1	2	3	4	5	6
1985-86	330	166481	85702	135492	387675
1986-87	329	149805	10635	165618	326058
1987-88	322	146982	114086	196210	457278
1988-89	320	161547	146188	268476	576211
1989-90	325	152614	157497	306666	616777
1990-91	325	144931	167697	307959	620587
1991-92	325	137299	149275	267879	554953
1992-93	325	127608	144527	271878	544013
1993-94	238	128246	161285	369029	658560

Source: Calculated from the data available in Statistical Abstracts of Orissa, 1979, 1981, 1991 and 1996, Govt. of Orissa.

Note: 1970-71 to 1988-89 excludes oral pill users.

Table—2.13: Effective couples protection rate (CPR) due to all methods as on 31st March in India and Orissa

Country/ State	*1980*	*1985*	*1990*	*1991*	*1992*	*1993*	*1994*	*1995*	*1996*	*1997*	*1998*	*1999*
India	22.3	32.1	43.3	44.1	43.6	43.5	45.4	45.8	46.5	45.4	45.4	48.6
Orissa	26.9	32.8	40.7	41.0	40.2	38.1	39.0	40.6	40.6	39.5	39.0	41.9

Source: Selected Socio-Economic Statistics, India, 1999, p. 45 Central Statistical Organisation, GoI. New Delhi.

Table—2.14: Sex-wise break-up of sterilization performed

Year	*No. of sterilization*			*Percentage of tubectomies to total*
	Vasectomy	*Tubectomy*	*Total*	
(1)	*(2)*	*(3)*	*(4)*	*(5)*
1980-81	438909	1613861	2052770	78.6
1985-86	639477	4262132	4901609	87.0
1990-91	254905	3870650	4125555	93.8
1991-92	174201	3915838	4090039	95.7
1992-93	150719	4135587	42866306	96.5

(Contd...)

1	2	3	4	5
1993-94	150235	4347215	4497450	96.7
1994-95	143866	4435648	4579514	96.9
1995-96	123748	4298571	4422319	97.2
1996-97	72023	3798203	3870226	98.1

Source: Year Book on Family Welfare Programme in India, 1996-97, p. 100, Dept. of Family Welfare, Ministry of Health and Family Welfare, GoI. New Delhi.

CHAPTER–III

Physical Characteristics and Social Structure of Study Villages and Slums

The study villages of this piece of research work constitute five caste Hindu villages, namely Kalarahanga, Raghunathpur, Daruthenga, Barimunda and Khairapada, and two slums, of Bhubaneswar city, namely Patharabandha and Salia Sahi. While all the five villages are located on the vicinity of Bhubaneswar city, the state capital of Orissa, both the slums are situated within the municipal boundary of the city. All these villages and slums fall within the Bhubaneswar block and belong to the district of Khordha of the state of Orissa.

From amongst the study villages, Khariapada and Barimunda are located on the north-east corner, Daruthenga on the north-west corner and the rest two villages, viz. Raghunathpur and Kalarahanga on the northern side of Bhubaneswar. These villages are located within an approximate distance of about 2-8 kilometres away from the nearest municipal boundary in the above direction of the concerned city. Both the slums are located on north side of the city taking state secretariat as the central point.

Basic Amenities and Infrastructure

Since all the study villages are located on the outskirts of Bhubaneswar city, the state capital of Orissa, these are well connected with either pucca or kutcha roads. However, the villages, namely Raghunathpur, Kalarahanga, Daruthenga are well connected with pucca through which bus service is presently available for the inhabitants of these villages. The other two villages, viz. Barimunda and Khairapada are connected with pucca roads to some extent but are well connected with developed kutcha roads and hence are easily approachable by four wheelers. However, residents of these villages are little away from the bus terminals. People of all these villages have easy access to Bhubaneswar as well as Cuttack and other places of the state.

Availability of educational facilities within the village area on at an approachable distance is considered as an important indicator of development. As a result, where there is lack of such facility, there has been less scope for development of the local people. But since all the study villages are located near the state capital the inhabitants of these villages have been enjoying better educational facilities beginning from primary to college and university levels. In each village, as shown in Table No. 3.1, there is a primary school. High school education is also available for the residents of all these villages. There are some colleges located in the area in which the people of the study villages have studied, and now, their children are being educated. The year of establishment of different educational institutions and their distance from the study villages are mentioned in the said table. It is learnt from the available data, that primary education is available within all the study villages.

So far as the medical and family health care facilities are concerned, the people of these villages normally depend on the local public health centres (PHCs) for curing of minor ailments and diseases but for the major ones, they mainly depend on the capital hospital located in unit-6 of Bhubaneswar city. Apart from this hospital, they also depend on other government hospitals, private clinics, nursing homes located at different points of the city. However, many people of the villages, like Khairapada and Barimuda depend on the hospitals and similar public health institutions located in Cuttack city since these two villages are situated at a middle place in-between Cuttack and Bhubaneswar cities.

As found from the said tables, the nearest public health centre is located at Patia for the village Kalarahanga (2 km), Baranga for Raghunathpur (6 km) and Khariapada (5 km), Gandarpur for Barimunda (4 km) and Mendhasal for Daruthenga (7 kms). At these health centres, the people of these villages normally undergo medical treatment for various diseases, family planning operations during camp movement and take advice of medical and family planning experts on birth control measures. But many come to take such help and assistance from the most reliable family welfare centre located in capital hospital.

As mentioned earlier the two slums, viz Patharabandha and Salia Sahi of our study are located inside the city in prime localities. Hence the communications facility to these slums is excellent and thus the residents of these slums have better access to different places as compared to those of study villages located around the city.

There is not a single permanent educational institution in any of these slums run by the government but some nursery and pre-nursery schools are there, which are being operated by some local NGOs. However, since these slums are located inside the city, the people of these slums have better opportunities for educating themselves as well as their children in various lower and higher educational institutions located around their habitations but most of them cannot avail these opportunities because of their poor economic condition and low level of awareness. Similarly there is no permanent medical institution inside their habitations. Still then they have better scope of availing medical and family welfare facilities from the local hospitals, public health centres or from any private clinic, nursing homes etc. But unfortunately there are very few persons who take the advantage of such resources as majority of people residing in such slums are poor, who primarily work as daily labourers, rickshaw pullers, petty vendors etc. and have no time to go to the hospital where they are to wait in a long queue for getting an appointment with the doctor or any other such practitioner. Moreover, they are educationally very backward and their awareness level about the benefits of having small families by adopting modern birth control measures is very very limited.

Households, Population Size and Sex Ratio

Data relating to village-wise households, total male and female population and average household size in the study villages and slums are presented in Table No. 3.1. It indicates that of all the study villages, Daruthenga consists of highest number of households followed by Raghunathpur, Kalarahanga, Barimunda and Kharipada, which have a total number of 454, 323, 312 and 79 households respectively.

Since the village Daruthenga consists of highest number of households it has also highest number of population (2852) as compared to other villages, e.g. Raghunathpur (2564), Barimunda (2094), Kalarahanga (1985) and Khariapada (502). But so far as the average household size of these villages is concerned, it is found that it is maximum in case of the village Barimunda which comes to be 6.71. This means that on an average each household of this village has approximately 7 persons irrespective of sex. This size seems to be quite high. Similarly, the average household size of the villages, like Khairapada and Kalarahanga are found to be quite high. i.e., more than 6 persons but less than 7 persons per household. It is only the village Daruthenga which has 5 persons on an average per household. The village Raghunathpur has however, an average household size of 5.65.

From the above discussion one more important revelation comes out into the fore. It is that even if the village Khairapada has lowest number of households and population as compared to the total households and population of other study villages, the average household size seems to be very high, which is 6.35.

Sex ratio is a very important indicator in demographic studies. It helps in understanding the population trend through sexual division. As in the Indian context, the proportion of males to the proportion of females has always remained more, in the present study the situation is also the same in case of all the study villages excepting Daruthenga which has a favourable sex ratio. This trend might be due to various reasons as discussed in the earlier chapter.

So far as the case of slums is concerned, the data available in Bhubaneswar Municipal Corporation (1997) point out that there are as many as 1013 households in Patharabandha as against 517 households in Salia Sahi. The former slum has a total number of 3834 population and the latter one consists of 1747 population irrespective of sex. Thus while the average household size of Patharabandha comes to be nearly 4 per household (3.79), it is 3 (3.38) for Salia Sahi. The male and female population figures are not available for these slums.

Social Category, Castes Composition and Inter Caste Relationship

Indian social organisation is based on the varna organisation and the most important aspect of the caste Hindu villages located in the coastal districts of Orissa is that, in most of such villages two broad social category of people reside together with approved social distance depending upon the rules of purity and population of caste occupations. These two broad social groups are: (i) Savarna or general castes belonging to varna order, i.e. Brahman (priest), Kshyatriya (ruling caste or militia), Vaishya (trader) and Shudra (artisan and ritual service castes), and (ii) Asavarna/Avarna who are officially designated as ex-untouchables/Scheduled Castes or those who are outside the pale of the varna organisation. In other districts, apart from these two broad social categories of people, another category of people residing in hilly and forest areas are found who are etymologically termed as Vanyaja, Vanyajati, Girijana etc. who have been scheduled and are popularly known as Scheduled Tribes.

Since all the study villages are located in a coastal district, i.e. Khurdha of Orissa, these villages normally comprise general belonging to varna order and Scheduled Castes who do not belong to these orders. There is not a single village which includes any Scheduled Tribe household excepting the village Raghunathpur. This village has a total umber of 26 Scheduled Tribe households (5.80%) who have immigrated from tribal districts and settled down here with a hope of earning regular livelihood through wage-earning, rickshaw pulling etc. in Bhubaneswar or in the adjoining areas of this city.

Scheduled Castes are an integral part of the caste Hindu villages. Hence, of the total villages studied, there are 3 villages, namely Raghunathpur, Barimunda and Kalarahanga each of which has more than 20 per cent Scheduled Caste households and each of the rest villages, like Khariapada and Daruthenga has less than 20 per cent but more than 17 per cent such households. As mentioned above, the village Raghunathpur comprises a total number of 26 tribal households which is 5.80 per cent of the total households of the village. These households have immigrated to this village as it is located close to Bhubaneswar city. The rest households of each village are all occupied by the general castes (Table 3.3).

So far as the caste composition of the study villages is concerned, each one is multi-ethnic and hence heterogeneous in nature.

From amongst the above villages, Daruthenga is found to have constituted the highest number of castes, i.e. 17 caste communities. Of these, 13 (76.47%) are general castes and the rest 5 (29.41%) are Scheduled Caste communities. This village is followed by the villages of Raghunathpur and Kalarahanga, having 15 castes each. But while the latter village has 11 (73.33%) number of general castes, it is 10 (66.67%) in case of the former one. The rest 4 (26.67%) castes of the village Kalarahanga belong to Scheduled Caste communities. There are 4 (26.67%) Scheduled Caste and 1 (6.67%) Scheduled Tribe household in the village Raghunathpur.

The village Barimunda comprises 14 caste communities of which 9 (64.29%) belong to general castes and the rest 5 (35.71%) are Scheduled Castes.

In all the study villages, excepting the village of Raghunathpur, the Bauris a major Scheduled Caste community who work as agricultural labourers, are found to be numerically preponderant as compared to other Scheduled Caste communities residing in these villages. In Raghunathpur the Keuta or fishermen constitute 66 households and the Bauris comprise 49 (10.94%) households. In other villages, like Kalarahanga, Daruthenga and Barimunda the Bauris reside in

54, 50 and 24 households, which constitute 15.67, 11.76 and 10.76 per cent respectively of the total households in the concerned villages.

So far as the numerical strength of individual general castes is concerned, it is found that among the general caste categories the Chasa or agricultural caste (33.48%) in Raghunathpur, Gauda or milkman (28.84%) in Kalarahanga, Brahman or priest (25.56%) in Barimunda and Khandayat or militia group (23.31%) in Daruthenga dominate the village population (Table 3.4). But socially the Brahmans are found to be most important and influential in all the villages. As economy plays a vital role in status identification and as Jajmani system is still prevalent in rural Orissa a different picture appears. In Raghunathpur and Daruthenga the Khandayats dominate the whole village as ownership of most of the landed properties remain with them. However, in other villages, like Kalarahanga and Barimunda, the Brahmans are considered both social as well as economically important.

However, in all the villages, the inter caste relationship is harmonious even though these villages are located around the fringes of the state capital and are under the high pressure of urbanisation. In these villages interaction among different caste communities mainly depends on the caste occupations, ritual purity and economic status of the castes. Hence, as pointed out in all the villages the Brahman occupy the top-most position in the Varna vyavastha of Indian social order and are ritually considered as superior to all others and enjoy the privilege of mediating between the human beings and the supernatural powers. Nowadays most of them have become educated and have become economically sound and thus have the ability to employ the local Scheduled Castes, preferably the Bauris as their agricultural labourers. The Khandayats were initially assigned the duty of physically protecting the Kingdom of past rulers and on victory they were gifted with landed properties by such rulers or kings. Their position, thus was very respectable in the society as they practised a prestigious occupation and at the same time they possessed enough landed property and thus controlled the management of the village in their hands.

The Chasa caste people are those who are engaged in farming in the past but nowadays they have sufficiently lost their properties and work in other sectors. The Bauris, were considered as an untouchable caste. However, in all the villages they occupy a higher social position as compared to other Dalit Caste communities in the study villages. They occupy a high social position among other Scheduled Caste communities because they do not practise any profane and lowly occupation. They work as agricultural labourers in the field of Brahman, Khandayat, Chasa people etc. and blow conch shell during ceremonial and ritual occasions. However, they are treated as untouchable since their food habit is considered as ritually unclean.

The caste composition in slums, total households, and percentage to total households are presented in Table No. 3.5. It is found that there are as many as 29 caste communities belonging to different social strata of the Indian social order. Of these, there are 15 General Castes, 8 Scheduled Castes and the rest 6 are Scheduled Tribe communities who constitute 57.19, 30.77 and 23.68 per cent respectively of the total caste living in Patharabandha slum. Apart from these 29 caste communities, there are 5 other categories of population who are unclassified. They are: Bihari, Bengali, Muslim, Telugu and Nepali.

The major Scheduled Tribes residing in this slum are: Kolha (198 households with 18.71%), Santal (84 households with 7.94%), and Munda (16 households with 1.51%) and the major Scheduled Caste of this slum are: Hadi or scavenger (105 households with 9.92%), Keuta or fishermen (14 households with 1.32%), and Kandara or village watch man (12 households with 1.13%). Among the general castes, Chasa or farmers are found with 106 households (10.2%), Khandayat or militia with 99 households (9.36%), Gauda or milkman with 89 households (8.41%), Karan or scribe with 35 households (3.31%), Badhei or carpenter with 32 households (3.02%), Brahman or priest with 28 households (2.65%), Kamara or blacksmith with 14 households (1.32%), Teli or oil crusher with 12 households (1.13%), Barika or barber and Kansari or brazier with 11 households (1.04%) each. Each one is found to be numerically preponderant whose share falls in-between 1 and 11 per cent households of the total 1058 households of the said slum (Table 3.5). Such figures are not available for Salia Sahi slum.

As mentioned earlier, each and every caste of Indian social system has its own social and economic importance, since different occupations have been specified for different castes. For the sake of smooth functioning of the village community or the society as a whole, each caste has to function in a particular order specified by the tradition and thus one caste is dependent on the other. This caste inter dependence is socially recognised depending upon the caste occupations, and the caste hierarchy is stratified depending on them. As a result, in each Indian village, there are some superior and some inferior or socially lower castes. The people of lower caste communities are to behave in a particular manner. They must respect and keep social distance from the upper caste depending upon the purity and pollution attached to them. However, these caste norms are very rigid in traditional village organisations, but they are not so in urban centres, particularly in slum settlements. Here the caste norms are very flexible.

However, as per the prevailing caste norms, a Brahman cannot take any type of food; it pucca or Kutcha from a Harijan household. But, here, in slums, a poor Brahman who has left his village and settled down in a slum, is quite free to render priestly service to a Hadi (scavenger) and earn his livelihood since there is no caste panchayat to look after the ritual duties of individual persons or castes.

Table—3.1: Educational and medical facilities available in study villages

Sl. No.	*Village*	*Educational institutions*	*Year of establishment*	*Appx. distance from the village (in km)*	*Nearest public health centres (PHCs)*	*App. distance from the village (in kms)*	*Nearest hospital*	*Appox. distance from the village*
(1)	(2)	(3)	(4)	(5)	(6)	(7)	(8)	(9)
1.	Kalarahanga	Kalarahanga centre primary school	1910	0	Patia	2 kms.	Unit-6 BBSR	11 km
2.	Raghunathpur	Raghunathapur U.G.M.E. School,	1917	0	Baranga	6 kms.	Unit-6 BBSR	15 km
		Dadhiban High School	1997	0				
		Kunjabihari Mahavidyalaya Baranga	1978	6				
3.	Khairapada	Khariapada Primary School	1903	0	Baranga	5 kms.	Unit-6 BBSR	20 km
		Utkalmani Ucha Vidyapitha,	1988	0			S.C.B Medical College, Cuttack	20 km
		Utkalamani Balika Ucha Vidyapitha,	1988	0				
		Barang Collge, Barang	–	4				
4.	Barimunda	Barimunda L.P. School,	1914	0	Gandarpur	4 kms.	Unit-6 BBSR	22 km
		Barimunda M.E. School,	1965	0			S.C.B Medical College, Cuttack	
		Bapujee Vidyapitha	1981	0				
5.	Daruthenga	Daruthenga U.P. School	1914	0	Mendasal	7 kms.	Unit-6 BBSR	25 km
		Daruthenga M.E. School	1962	0				
		Daruthenga high school	1984	0				
		Jujhagada primary school	1962	0				
		Kunjabihari Mahavidyalaya	1978	7				

Table—3.2: Population profile of the study villages and slums

Sl. No.	Village/ slum	Total households	Population Male	Female	Total	Average household size
(1)	(2)	(3)	(4)	(5)	(6)	(7)
1.	Kalarahanga	323	1019 (51.34)	966 (48.66)	1985 (100.00)	6.15
2.	Raghunathpur	454	1306 (50.94)	1258 (49.06)	2564 (100.00)	5.65
3.	Khairapada	76	255 (50.80)	247 (49.20)	502 (100.00)	6.35
4.	Barimunda	312	1057 (50.48)	1037 (49.52)	2094 (100.00)	6.71
5.	Daruthenga	551	1424 (49.93)	1428 (50.07)	2852 (100.00)	5.18
6.	Patharabandha (slum)	1013	NA	NA	3834 (100.00)	3.79
7.	Salia Sahi (slum)	517	NA	NA	1747 (100.00)	3.38

Note: Figures in brackets represent percentage.

Source: *(i)* From Sl. No. 1-5, Village Census Abstracts, Bhubaneswar block (un published) Census of India, Bhubaneswar.

(ii) From Sl. No. 6-7, Bhubaneswar Municipal Corporation, 1997.

Table—3.3: Study villages according to social category of population

Sl. No.	Village/slum	Category of population (in HHs) SC	ST	OC	Total
(1)	(2)	(3)	(4)	(5)	(6)
1.	Kalarahanga	66 (20.69)	–	253 (79.31)	319 (100.00)
2.	Raghunathpur	121 (27.01)	26 (5.80)	301 (67.19)	448 (100.00)
3.	Khairapada	15 (18.99)	–	64 (81.01)	79 (100.00)

(Contd...)

(1)	*(2)*	*(3)*	*(4)*	*(5)*	*(6)*
4.	Barimunda	58 (26.01)	–	165 (73.99)	223 (100.00)
5.	Daruthenga	79 (17.21)	–	380 (82.79)	459 (100.00)
6.	Patharabandha (slum)	183 (17.30)	297 (28.07)	578 (54.63)	1058 (100.00)
7.	Salia Sahi (slum)	–	–	–	517 (100.00)

Note: Figures in brackets represent percentage.

Source: *(i)* From 1-5, Local Panchayat Office.

(ii) Data in Sl. No. 6 from the Secretary Patharabandha slum, 1999.

Table—3.4: Caste composition in study villages according to households

Sl. No.	*Castes*	*Villages*				
		Raghu-nathpur	*Kalara-hanga*	*Bari-munda*	*Khaira-pada*	*Daru-thenga*
(1)	(2)	(3)	(4)	(5)	(6)	(7)
A.	**General castes**					
1.	Badhei (Carpenter)	–	7 (2.19)	–	NA	6 (1.31)
2.	Barika (Barber)	2 (0.45)	13 (4.08)	13 (5.83)	–	14 (3.05)
3.	Brahmin (Priest)	23 (5.13)	51 (15.99)	57 (25.56)	–	20 (4.36)
4.	Chasa (Agriculturist)	150 (33.48)	33 (10.34)	40 (17.94)	–	101 (22.00)
5.	Gauda (Milkman)	7 (1.56)	92 (28.84)	12 (5.38)	–	9 (1.96)
6.	Gudia (Confectioner)	25 (5.58)	10 (3.13)	1 (0.45)	–	4 (0.87)
7.	Jyotish (Astrologer)	2 (0.45)	10 (3.13)	–	–	1 (0.22)
8.	Kamara (Blacksmith)	2 (0.45)	–	1 (0.45)	–	2 (0.44)

(Contd...)

(1)	(2)	(3)	(4)	(5)	(6)	(7)
9.	Karana (Scribe)	4 (0.89)	1 (0.31)	–	–	32 (6.97)
10.	Khandayat (Militia)	83 (18.53)	8 (2.51)	10 (4.48)	–	107 (23.31)
11.	Mali (Flowerist)	–	–	–	–	10 (2.18)
12.	Patra (Petty trader)	–	–	18 (8.07)	–	–
13.	Tanti (Weaver)	–	19 (5.96)	–	–	6
14.	Teli (Oil crusher)	3 (0.67)	9 (2.82)	8 (3.59)	–	67 (14.60)
	Sub-total	**301 (67.19)**	**253 (79.31)**	**165 (73.99)**	–	**380 (82.79)**
B.	**Scheduled Castes**					
1.	Bauri (Conch shell blower)	49 (10.94)	50 (15.67)	24 (10.76)	–	54 (11.76)
2.	Dhoba (Washerman)	4 (0.89)	4 (1.25)	4 (1.79)	–	5 (1.09)
3.	Dom (Hider)	–	–	13 (5.83)	–	–
4.	Hadi (Nightsoil (remover)	2 (0.45)	2 (0.63)	–	–	2 (0.44)
5.	Kandara (Village watchman)	–	–	10 (4.48)	–	–
6.	Keuta (Fisherman)	66 (14.73)	10 (3.13)	7 (3.14)	–	18 (3.92)
	Sub-total	**121 (27.01)**	**66 (20.69)**	**58 (26.01)**	–	**79 (17.21)**
C.	**Scheduled Tribes**					
1.	Savara	26 (5.80)	–	–	–	–
	Total	**448 (100.00)**	**319 (100.00)**	**223 (100.00)**	**79 (100.00)**	**459 (100.00)**

Note: (*i*) Figures in brackets represent percentage

(*ii*) Caste-wise data are not available for the village Khairapada.

Source: Local Panchayat Office.

Table—3.5: Caste composition study slums (Patharabandha) according to households

Sl. No.	Castes	Total households	Percentage
(1)	(2)	(3)	(4)
A.	Ocs		
1.	Badhei (Carpenter)	32	3.02
2.	Bania (Gold smith)	5	0.42
3.	Barik (Barber)	11	1.04
4.	Brahman (Priest)	28	2.65
5.	Chasa (Agriculturist)	106	10.2
6.	Gaudier (Milk man)	89	8.41
7.	Kachra (Bangla seller)	1	0.95
8.	Kamara (Blacksmith)	14	1.32
9.	Kansari (Brazier)	11	1.04
10.	Karana (Scribe)	35	3.31
11.	Khandayat (Militia)	99	9.36
12.	Mali (Flowerist)	6	0.57
13.	Patra (Petty Trader)	1	0.95
14.	Tanti (Weaver)	6	0.57
15.	Teli (Oil crusher)	12	1.13
	Sub-total	**456**	**43.10**
B.	SCs		
1.	Bauri (Conch shell blower)	9	0.95
2.	Dhoba (Washer man)	10	0.95
3.	Hadi (Nightsoil remover)	105	9.92
4.	Kandara (Village watchman)	12	1.13
5.	Keuta (Fisherman)	14	1.32
6.	Kumbhara (Potter)	7	0.66
7.	Pana (Drum beater)	22	2.08
8.	Sundhi (Toddy maker)	4	0.38
	Sub-total	**183**	**17.30**

(Contd...)

(1)	*(2)*	*(3)*	*(4)*
C.	**STs**		
1.	Bathudi	1	0.95
2.	Ho	1	0.95
3.	Kolha	198	18.71
4.	Munda	16	1.51
5.	Sabara	5	0.47
6.	Santal	84	7.94
	Sub-total	**305**	**28.82**
D.	**Unclassified**		
1.	Bihari	10	0.95
2.	Bengali	2	0.19
3.	Muslim	8	0.76
4.	Telugu	87	8.22
5.	Nepali	7	0.66
	Sub-total	**114**	**10.78**
	Total	**1058**	**100.00**

Source: Secretary, Patharabandha (as per the survey conducted on 2.11.99).

CHAPTER—IV

Demographic Profile of the Ethnic Communities

Demography is an important discipline in population science. It deals with various important statistics, like fertility, mortality, disease, age and sex ratio, educational status, nature of occupations etc. of different communities. As such, depending on these statistics evaluation is made, development planning is formulated and future profile is forecasted. Therefore, it is necessary to discuss some of such vital aspects relating to the ethnic groups studied before we deal with the result of this piece of research work.

Distribution of Ethnic Groups by Population, Age and Sex

Data relating to caste-wise population size, age and sex ratio etc. are presented in Table No. 4.1. It is observed that from amongst the 4 caste communities, the Chasa have the highest size of population, in 265 as compared to 247 Bauri, 246 Brahman and 239 Santal people. Of the total population of each community, excepting the Brahman, the male outnumber the female population. In case of the Brahman community the male population constitutes 49.59 per cent of the total population, thereby indicating the share of female population to be 50.41 per cent. Among the Bauri, Santal and Chasa the male population accounts for 55.44, 51.88 and 52.08 per cent respectively of the total population of each community. The rest are female population. If one looks at the grand total figures, the trend is observed to be the same as of the whole population of 997 persons, 521 or 52.26 per cent are male and the rest 476 or 47.74 per cent are female.

So far as the age group-wise population profile of each caste community is concerned, about 15.5 per cent of the total Santal population are found to be in the age group of 0-4. They are followed by 10.12 per cent of Bauri, 8.54 per cent of Brahman and 5.66 per cent of Chasa in this age group. Hence, it is found that the Santal people have more number of infants and children compared to other caste communities. But in the next two age groups, viz 5-9 and 10-19 in which children normally receive education, about 43 per cent of Chasa are concentrated as against 39 per cent of Bauri, 35 per cent of Santal and 27 per cent of Brahmans. Next to these age groups, in the age groups of 20-29, 30-39 and 40-49 which are considered as the most important reproductive age groups, altogether 50 per cent of Brahman are found in this group and are followed by Chasa and Santal, each having 44 per cent of population. The Bauri constitute about 39 per cent of the total population belonging to these age groups.

The age groups of 50-59 is considered as the transitional phase in-between reproductive age group and old age, and hence this age group has a special significance. The percentage of people falling in this age group when compared with the total population of each caste community is found to be the highest (4.60) for Santal as against 4.45 of Bauri, 4.28 of Brahman and 3.77 of Chasa. The percentage of Brahmans (8.94) in the last age group, i.e. 60+ is more, as compared to 3.02 of Chasa, 2.83 of Bauri and only 1.26 of Santals (Table No. 4.1).

So far as the age groups of female spouse are concerned, it is observed from the Table No. 4.2 that irrespective of any caste community, most of the women (24.00%) are found in the age group of 25-29. They are followed by 19 per cent in the age group of 25-29, 17 per cent in the age group of 30-34, and 14.5 per cent in the age group of 20-24. In the last two age groups, viz 40-44 and 45-49, altogether there are 18.5 per cent female spouses. The first reproductive age group which is 15-19 constitutes only 6 per cent (Table 4.2) of female spouses as the people have become more conscious and hence do not arrange marriage of their daughters at this young age. However, the number of female spouses among the Santal and Bauri is more as compared to the Brahman and Chasa people who are found to have married at this early age. However, this happens mainly because, the former primarily depend on wage-earning and in that condition they do not like to spend more and more money on the maintenance of their daughters by delaying their marriage. Moreover, in these communities the females are considered as economic assets who often earn their own bread and butter. Apart from these facts there is also another important reason for this phenomenon. Since educationally these people are very backward, their awareness about the bad effects of early marriage is very limited. They still consider a girl who has attained puberty as eligible for marriage and for this, keeping a girl with parents for long time after her puberty is not generally appreciated in the society. If, at all such a girl is kept for a long period with her parents, both the parents as well as the concerned girl are humiliated.

Communities and Family Types

Data available in Table 4.3 indicate the types of family among the four communities studied. It is found that out of the total of 50 households of each community, highest percentage (94.00) of Brahman households are having vertically extended family followed by 38 per cent of nuclear and 18 per cent of supplemented households. But among the rest 3 communities, viz Chasa, Bauri and Santal, most of the households belong to nuclear type. The number of this type of households come to 30 (60.00%) of the Chasa, 27 (54.00%) for the Bauri and 35 (75.00%) for the Santal. The total figures reveal that irrespective of communities, highest number of households, i.e. 111 or 55.5 per cent are of nuclear type, 54 or 27.00 per cent are of vertically extended type and the rest 35 or 17.5 per cent are of supplemented type. Thus, there is not a single household among any of the above caste communities which is horizontally extended. This is because the people have become individualistic, possessive of material objects for personal satisfaction and also because the old values are dwelling away fast over the last few decades; both in sub-urban as well as rural areas.

Distribution of Population according to Ethnic Groups and Educational Status

The educational status of the sample population is presented in Table No. 4.4, 4.5, 4.6 and 4.7. The first table indicates the educational status of the whole population of each caste community only by dual break-up, viz literate and illiterate. The next table focuses on the education of these people by different educational levels. The succeeding two tables have been devoted for presenting the educational status of the male and female spouses in each community, as literate, illiterate and assorted educational levels.

It can be observed from the data available in Table No. 4.4 that of the four communities, educationally Brahmans are found to be most advanced irrespective of sex. As many as 181 or 80.44 per cent of the total of 225 persons of this community are literate as against 131 or 52.40 per cent of Chasa, 96 or 43.24 per cent of Bauri and 84 or 41.58 per cent of Santal. This otherwise reveals that fact that more number of Santals are illiterate as compared to Bauri, Chasa and Brahman. Another important fact which is revealed from this table is that in case of all the communities, the rate of literacy of women is much lower than their male counterparts. It comes to 69.37 per cent as against 91.23 per cent of males in Brahman community followed by 42.86 per cent women as against 61.17 per cent males in Chasa community. For the Bauri community, it is 24.74 per cent for the women and 57.60 per cent for the men. But for the Santal, it is 28.42 per cent for the women as against 53.27 per cent men. Thus, female population of Santal community is found to be little more educated than those of the Bauri. This higher trend of literacy of the female population of Santal community might be due to better educational opportunities available to them in the city and also because of higher impact of urbanisation and modernisation.

As to the educational levels achieved by the literate persons. It can be said that there are 9 or 4 per cent of Brahmans who are Master-degree holders but surprisingly this level has not been achieved by any person of the rest three communities. Moreover, there are as many as 27 persons in Brahman community who have completed Graduation level education. They are followed by only 3 or 1.2 per cent of Chasas and 2 or 0.9 per cent of Bauris who are found to have completed this level of education. But there is not a single person in Santal community who is graduate. The level of education among the rest of the literate persons of each community fall in-between primary and +2 level. Further, it is also observed that in higher educational levels, that is, Matriculation and above, the percentage of females is comparatively much lower than the males of each community studied (Table 4.5).

Educational status of the male and female informants of each community follows more or less the same trend as that of the total population and thus, the rate of literacy among female spouses of each community is found to be less as compared to the literacy rate of their male counterparts. However, while the literacy rate of all the females of Brahman community is found to be 66 per cent as against 88 per cent of all their male spouses, it is only 32 per cent for the Chasa female spouses as against 58 per cent of their male spouses. The level of literacy of Bauri and Santal female spouses are found to be 20 and 12 per cent respectively as against 52 per cent of Bauri and 42 per cent of Santal male spouses. The total figures show that irrespective of any caste community there are only 32.5 per cent of female spouses as against 60 per cent male spouses who are literate (Table 4.6).

The educational levels compared by the male and female spouses are mentioned in the Table No. 4.7. Of the total 200 female spouses of all the communities taken together, there are 10 or 5 per cent of female spouses as against 23 or 11.50 per cent of male spouses who have completed high school education. The percentage of those who have completed +2 level comes to only 2 in case of the female spouses and 6 for the male spouses. However, there are 3 (1.5%) female spouses as against 15 (7.5%) male spouses who have completed graduation. But there is not a single female spouse who is found to have passed Master degree but there are 2 (1.00) male spouses who are educated upto this level. However, the community-wise figures suggest that while the education of female spouses ranges upto graduation level in case of the Brahman and Chasa communities, the level of education of female spouses of Bauri community ranges only upto matriculation and it remains within high school level for the Santals.

Distribution of Households by Occupation

Caste and occupation are two interrelated concepts. Based on this, one's occupation is predominantly determined by its caste membership in a caste ridden rural Indian society. But due to the tremendous advancement in the level of education and modernisation among the people, caste norms have more or less become redundant and many people have drifted away from their own caste occupations. But it has not yet been possible among the lower castes because of their economic and educational backwardness and the fear of facing rigid social sanctions imposed by the society. Still then many households belonging to such castes are seen to have taken to various non-traditional or white-collar jobs. As a result of this in the present study, people of different ethnic communities are found to have taken to different modern jobs which are profitable to them.

The traditional caste occupation of Brahmans is to worship divinities and render priestly services to the people belonging to other castes. The Chasa are the traditional agricultural caste and the Bauris work as agricultural labourers and wage-earners. They also blow conch shell as their caste occupation and they render their services to various castes during various ceremonies, festive occasions and rituals. The Santal, being a forest dwelling tribal community did not have any specific occupation rather they were earning their livelihood from the forest as hunters and food gatherers and also from crude farming. But now-a-days these people have become quite modernised compared to other tribal communities and are found to be migrating to different industrial and urban areas to work as common wage-labourers and construction workers.

Of the total 50 sample households of each community, the Brahman households are found to earn their livelihood from as many as 7 types of occupation, viz. agriculture (31 or 62.00%), salaried service in public sector institutions (7 or 14.00%), shop-keeping and service in private sector institutions (3 or 6.00% each), driving of motor vehicles (1 or 2.00%) and prescribing health care services to the public as quacks (1 or 2.00%). The rest 3 or 6 per cent households earn their daily bread out of their own caste occupation, i.e. by rendering priestly service to the eligible households and as traditional cook during festive and ceremonial occasions. The Chasas earn their livelihood from 9 types of occupation. These are: agriculture (19 or 38.0%), share cropping (10 or 20%), shop keeping (6 or 12%) working in private sector institutions (4 or 8%), providing contact labourers as petty contractors (3 or 6.00%), masonry (2 or 4.00%), salaried service in public sector institutions (2 or 4.00%), sale of vegetables (2 or 4.00%) and wage-labour (2 or 4.00%).

The Bauri households have adopted as many as 10 types of occupation, such as wage-earning, preferably as agricultural labourers (32 or 64.00%), rickshaw-pulling (4 or 8.00%), coconut plucking (3 or 6.00%), driving of motor vehicles (2 or 4.00%), salaried service in public sector institutions (2 or 4.00%), share-cropping (2 or 4.00%), salaried service in private sector institutions (2 or 4.00%), and private tuition (1 or 2.00%); and the households of the rest one community, in Santal have chosen 8 types of occupation for their livelihood. These are: wage-earning (26 or 52.00%), masonry (8 or 16.00%), rickshaw/trolley pulling (6 or 12.00%), salaried service in public sector institutions (4 or 8.00%), driving of motor vehicles and shop keeping (2 or 4.00% each), carpeting and service in private sector institutions (1 or 2.00 each). Thus, from these statistics, it is evident that most of the Brahman and Chasa households earn their livelihood primarily from agriculture but most of the households of Bauri and Santal communities depend on wage-earning for their daily bread and butter. The second important occupation from which quite a good number of households earn their livelihood, is found to be salaried service in public sector institutions for the Brahman, share-cropping for the Chasa, rickshaw and trolley pulling for Bauris and masonry work for the Santals (Table 4.8).

Table—4.1: Distribution of population according to age and sex

Age groups	Brahman			Chasa			Bauri			Santal			Total		
	M	F	T	M	F	T	M	F	T	M	F	T	M	F	T
(1)	(2)	(3)	(4)	(5)	(6)	(7)	(8)	(9)	(10)	(11)	(12)	(13)	(14)	(15)	(16)
0-4	8 (2.25)	13 (5.28)	21 (8.54)	7 (2.64)	8 (3.02)	15 (5.66)	12 (4.86)	13 (5.26)	25 (10.12)	17 (7.11)	20 (8.37)	37 (15.48)	44 (4.41)	54 (5.42)	98 (9.83)
5-9	10 (4.07)	10 (4.06)	20 (8.13)	15 (5.67)	15 (5.66)	30 (11.32)	20 (8.10)	8 (3.24)	28 (11.34)	19 (7.95)	18 (7.53)	37 (15.48)	64 (6.42)	51 (5.12)	115 (11.53)
10-19	23 (9.35)	24 (9.76)	47 (19.11)	42 (15.85)	42 (15.85)	84 (31.70)	41 (16.60)	27 (10.93)	68 (27.53)	25 (10.46)	21 (8.79)	46 (19.25)	131 (13.14)	114 (11.43)	245 (24.57)
20-29	18 (7.32)	28 (13.8)	46 (18.70)	18 (6.79)	15 (5.66)	33 (12.45)	23 (9.31)	22 (8.91)	45 (18.22)	15 (6.28)	24 (10.04)	39 (16.32)	74 (7.42)	89 (8.95)	163 (16.3)
30-39	24 (9.76)	23 (9.35)	47 (19.11)	19 (7.17)	25 (9.43)	44 (16.60)	10 (4.05)	22 (8.91)	32 (12.96)	24 (10.04)	18 (7.53)	42 (17.57)	77 (7.72)	88 (8.83)	165 (16.35)
40-49	19 (7.72)	11 (4.47)	30 (12.20)	25 (9.43)	16 (6.04)	41 (15.47)	21 (8.5)	10 (4.05)	31 (12.55)	14 (5.86)	10 (4.18)	24 (10.04)	79 (7.92)	47 (4.71)	126 (12.64)
50-59	9 (4.47)	4 (1.63)	13 (4.28)	7 (2.64)	3 (1.13)	10 (3.77)	8 (3.24)	3 (1.21)	11 (4.45)	9 (3.77)	2 (0.84)	11 (4.60)	33 (3.31)	12 (1.20)	45 (4.51)
60+	11 (4.47)	11 (4.47)	22 (8.94)	5 (1.89)	3 (1.13)	8 (3.02)	2 (0.81)	5 (2.02)	7 (2.83)	1 (0.42)	2 (0.84)	3 (1.26)	19 (1.91)	21 (2.11)	40 (4.01)
Total	**122 (49.59)**	**124 (50.41)**	**246 (100.00)**	**138 (52.08)**	**127 (47.92)**	**265 (100.00)**	**137 (55.44)**	**110 (44.53)**	**247 (100.00)**	**124 (51.88)**	**115 (48.12)**	**239 (100.00)**	**521 (52.26)**	**476 (47.74)**	**997 (100.00)**

Note: Figures in brackets represent percentage.

Table—4.2: Distribution of female spouses according to ethnic groups by age groups

Age groups	*Brahman*	*Chasa*	*Bauri*	*Santal*	*Total*
(1)	*(2)*	*(3)*	*(4)*	*(5)*	*(6)*
15-19	1 (2.00)	3 (6.00)	4 (8.00)	4 (8.00)	12 (6.0)
20-24	7 (14.00)	5 (10.00)	4 (8.00)	13 (26.00)	29 (14.5)
25-29	15 (30.00)	8 (16.00)	16 (32.00)	9 (18.00)	48 (24.00)
30-34	10 (20.00)	9 (18.00)	8 (16.00)	7 (14.00)	34 (17.00)
35-39	8 (16.00)	11 (22.00)	11 (22.00)	8 (16.00)	38 (19.00)
40-44	5 (10.00)	9 (18.00)	2 (4.00)	6 (12.00)	22 (11.00)
45-49	4 (8.00)	5 (10.00)	5 (10.00)	3 (6.00)	17 (8.5)
Total	**50 (100.00)**	**50 (100.00)**	**50 (100.00)**	**50 (100.00)**	**200 (100.00)**

Note: Figures in brackets represent percentage.

Table—4.3: Family types according to ethnic groups

Family types	*Brahman*	*Chasa*	*Bauri*	*Santal*	*Total*
(1)	*(2)*	*(3)*	*(4)*	*(5)*	*(6)*
Nuclear	19 (38.00)	30 (60.00)	27 (54.00)	35 (70.00)	111 (55.50)
Vertically extended	22 (44.00)	12 (24.00)	13 (26.00)	7 (14.00)	54 (27.00)
Supplemented	9 (18.00)	8 (16.00)	10 (20.00)	8 (16.00)	35 (17.00)
Total	**50 (100.00)**	**50 (100.00)**	**50 (100.00)**	**50 (100.00)**	**200 (100.00)**

Note: Figures in brackets represent percentage.

Table—4.4: Total literate and illiterate population according to ethnic groups

Variable	Brahman			Chasa			Bauri			Santal			Total		
	M	F	T	M	F	T	M	F	T	M	F	T	M	F	T
(1)	(2)	(3)	(4)	(5)	(6)	(7)	(8)	(9)	(10)	(11)	(12)	(13)	(14)	(15)	(16)
Literate	104 (91.23)	77 (69.37)	181 (80.44)	80 (61.07)	51 (42.86)	131 (52.40)	72 (57.60)	24 (24.74)	96 (43.24)	57 (53.27)	27 (28.42)	84 (41.58)	313 (65.62)	179 (42.42)	492 (54.73)
Illiterate	10 (8.77)	34 (30.63)	44 (19.56)	51 (38.93)	68 (57.14)	119 (47.60)	53 (42.40)	73 (75.26)	126 (56.76)	50 (46.73)	68 (71.58)	118 (58.42)	164 (34.38)	243 (57.358)	407 (45.27)
Total	**114 (1.00)**	**111 (100.00)**	**225 (100.00)**	**131 (100.00)**	**119 (100.00)**	**250 (100.00)**	**125 (100.00)**	**97 (100.00)**	**222 (100.00)**	**107 (100.00)**	**95 (100.00)**	**202 (100.00)**	**477 (100.00)**	**422 (100.00)**	**899 (100.00)**

Note: (i) Figures in brackets represent percentage.

(ii) Calculation has been made after deducting population falling in the age group of 0-4 from the total population.

Table—4.5: Educational status of total population according to ethnic groups

Educational levels	Brahman			Chasa			Bauri			Santal			Total		
	M	F	T	M	F	T	M	F	T	M	F	T	M	F	T
(1)	(2)	(3)	(4)	(5)	(6)	(7)	(8)	(9)	(10)	(11)	(12)	(13)	(14)	(15)	(16)
Illiterate	10 (8.77)	34 (30.63)	44 (19.56)	51 (38.93)	68 (57.14)	119 (47.6)	53 (42.4)	73 (75.26)	126 (56.76)	50 (46.73)	68 (71.58)	118 (58.42)	164 (34.38)	243 (57.58)	407 (45.27)
1st-5th	27 (23.68)	18 (16.22)	45 (20.0)	38 (29.01)	19 (15.97)	57 (22.80)	30 (24.0)	15 (15.46)	45 (20.27)	38 (35.51)	23 (24.21)	61 (30.20)	133 (27.88)	75 (17.77)	208 (23.14)
6th-10th	21 (18.42)	24 (21.62)	45 (20.0)	26 (19.85)	20 (16.81)	46 (18.40)	34 (27.2)	8 (8.25)	42 (18.92)	16 (14.95)	4 (4.21)	20 (9.90)	97 (20.34)	56 (13.27)	153 (17.02)
Matriculation	12 (10.53)	16 (14.41)	28 (12.44)	10 (7.63)	8 (6.72)	18 (7.20)	5 (4.0)	1 (1.03)	6 (2.70)	1 (0.93)	–	1 (0.50)	28 (5.87)	25 (5.92)	53 (5.90)
Secondary/+2	18 (15.79)	7 (6.31)	25 (11.11)	4 (3.05)	3 (2.52)	7 (2.80)	–	1 (0.45)	2 (1.87)	– 2	2 (1.0)	25 (5.24)	10 (2.37)	10 (2.37)	37 (4.12)
Graduation	16 (14.04)	11 (9.91)	27 (12.00)	2 (1.53)	1 (0.84)	3 (1.20)	2 (1.6)	–	2 (0.90)	–	–	–	20 (4.19)	12 (2.84)	32 (3.56)
Master degree	8 (7.02)	1 (0.9)	9 (4.0)	–	–	–	–	–	–	–	–	–	8 (1.68)	1 (0.24)	9 (1.00)
Technical	2 (1.75)	–	2 (0.9)	–	–	–	–	–	–	–	–	–	2 (0.42)	–	2 (0.22)
Total	**114 (100.00)**	**111 (100.00)**	**225 (100.00)**	**131 (100.00)**	**119 (100.00)**	**250 (100.00)**	**125 (100.00)**	**97 (100.00)**	**222 (100.00)**	**107 (100.00)**	**95 (100.00)**	**202 (100.00)**	**477 (100.00)**	**422 (100.00)**	**899 (100.00)**

Note: Figures in brackets represent percentage.

Table—4.6: Total literature and illiterate male and female spouses according to ethnic groups

	Brahman			Chasa			Bauri			Santal			Total		
Variables	*M*	*F*	*T*	*M*	*F*	*T*	*M*	*F*	*T*	*M*	*F*	*T*	*M*	*F*	*T*
(1)	*(2)*	*(3)*	*(4)*	*(5)*	*(6)*	*(7)*	*(8)*	*(9)*	*(10)*	*(11)*	*(12)*	*(13)*	*(14)*	*(15)*	*(16)*
Literate	44 (88.00)	33 (66.00)	27 (27.00)	29 (58.00)	16 (32.00)	45 (45.00)	26 (52.00)	10 (20.00)	36 (36.00)	21 (42.00)	6 (12.00)	27 (27.00)	120 (60.00)	65 (32.50)	185 (46.25)
Illiterate	6 (12.00)	17 (34.00)	23 (23.00)	21 (42.00)	34 (68.00)	55 (55.00)	24 (48.00)	40 (80.00)	64 (64.00)	29 (58.00)	44 (88.00)	73 (73.00)	80 (40.00)	135 (67.50)	215 (53.75)
Total	**50 (100.00)**	**50 (100.00)**	**100 (100.00)**	**50 (100.00)**	**50 (100.00)**	**100 (100.00)**	**50 (100.00)**	**50 (100.00)**	**100 (100.00)**	**50 (100.00)**	**50 (100.00)**	**100 (100.00)**	**200 (100.00)**	**200 (100.00)**	**400 (100.00)**

Note: Figures in brackets represent percentage.

Table—4.7: Educational status of male and female spouses according to ethnic groups

Educational levels	Brahman		Chasa		Bauri		Santal		Total	
	Male spouses	*Female spouses*	*Male spouses*	*Female spouses*	*Male spouses*	*Female spouses*	*Male spouses*	*Female spouses*	*Male spouses*	*Female spouses*
(1)	*(2)*	*(3)*	*(4)*	*(5)*	*(6)*	*(7)*	*(8)*	*(9)*	*(10)*	*(11)*
Illiterate	6 (12.00)	17 (34.00)	21 (42.00)	34 (68.00)	24 (48.00)	40 (80.00)	29 (58.00)	44 (88.00)	80 (40.00)	135 (67.50)
1st-5th	4 (8.00)	8 (16.00)	16 (32.00)	7 (14.00)	13 (26.00)	6 (12.00)	5 (10.00)	4 (8.00)	38 (19.00)	25 (12.50)
6th-10th	2 (4.00)	12 (24.00)	9 (18.00)	6 (12.00)	9 (18.00)	3 (6.00)	8 (16.00)	2 (4.00)	28 (14.00)	23 (11.50)
Matriculation	16 (32.00)	7 (14.00)	2 (4.00)	2 (4.00)	1 (2.00)	1 (2.00)	4 (8.00)	–	23 (11.50)	10 (5.00)
Intermediate	8 (16.00)	4 (8.00)	1 (2.00)	–	1 (2.00)	–	2 (4.00)	–	12 (6.00)	4 (2.00)
Graduation	10 (20.00)	2 (4.00)	1 (2.00)	1 (2.00)	2 (4.00)	–	2 (4.00)	–	15 (7.50)	3 (1.50)
Master degree	2 (4.00)	–	–	–	–	–	–	–	2 (1.00)	–
Technical	2 (4.00)	–	–	–	–	–	–	–	2 (1.00)	–
Total	**50 (100.00)**	**50 (100.00)**	**50 (100.00)**	**50 (100.00)**	**50 (100.00)**	**50 (100.00)**	**50 (100.00)**	**50 (100.00)**	**200 (100.00)**	**200 (100.00)**

Note: Figures in brackets represent percentage.

Table—4.8: Distribution of male informants according to occupation and ethnic groups

Sl. No.	*Occupation*	*Brahman*	*Chasa*	*Bauri*	*Santal*	*Total*
(1)	*(2)*	*(3)*	*(4)*	*(5)*	*(6)*	*(7)*
1.	Agriculture	31 (62.00)	19 (38.00)	–	–	50 (25.00)
2.	Coconut plucking	–	–	3 (6.00)	–	3 (1.50)
3.	Carpeting	–	–	–	1 (2.00)	1 (0.5)
4.	Driving and motor vehicles	1 (2.00)	–	2 (4.00)	2 (4.00)	5 (2.50)
5.	Elected panchayat workers	1 (2.00)	–	1 (2.00)	–	2 (1.00)
6.	Homeopathic quack	1 (2.00)	–	–	–	1 (0.50)
7.	Masonry	–	2 (4.00)	1 (2.00)	8 (16.00)	11 (5.50)
8.	Petty contractor	–	3 (6.00)	–	–	3 (1.50)
9.	Rickshaw/trolley pulling	–	–	4 (8.00)	6 (12.00)	10 (5.00)
10.	Service in public sector institutions	7 (14.00)	2 (4.00)	2 (4.00)	4 (8.00)	15 (7.50)

(Contd...)

(1)	(2)	(3)	(4)	(5)	(6)	(7)
11.	Share-cropping	–	10 (20.00)	2 (4.00)	–	12 (6.00)
12.	Shop-keeping	3 (6.00)	6 (12.00)	–	2 (4.00)	11 (5.50)
13.	Temporary worker in private sectors institutions	3 (6.00)	4 (8.00)	2 (4.00)	1 (2.00)	10 (5.00)
14.	Traditional cook/priest	3 (6.00)	–	–	–	3 (1.50)
15.	Tuition	–	–	1 (2.00)	–	1 (0.50)
16.	Vegetable selling	–	2 (4.00)	–	–	2 (1.00)
17.	Wage-earning	–	2 (4.00)	32 (64.00)	26 (52.00)	60 (30.00)
	Total	**50 (100.00)**	**50 (100.00)**	**50 (100.00)**	**50 (100.00)**	**200 (100.00)**

Note: Figures in brackets represent percentage.

CHAPTER–V

Modern Family Planning Devices and Methods

Traditionally, rural people in India plan their family through various indigenous methods. Some of such methods widely prevalent among them are: rhythm method and outside ejaculation of semen. But these methods are not completely safe for avoiding pregnancy. Because in the former method, the couple, particularly the female spouse, has to always remain alert as this method involves some mathematical calculation of time after and before commencement of menstruation. However, the efficacy of this method depends on the accuracy of calculation made. But the chances of miscalculation are very high if the monthly menstrual cycle is irregular. As such, if there is any deviation in calculating the safe period, there may be pregnancy. In this context Raina writes that "the conception takes place when ovum and sperm unite. If couples have sexual union during the period, ovum and sperm in the female genital tract are incapable of union, and conception will not take place. The calculation of safe period thus depends on the determination of the time when ovulation takes place and the period during which sperm and ovum are capable of successful union. It is generally assumed that ovum is released from the ovary 14-16 days before the onset of the next menstruation, the ovum can be fertilized upto 24 hours after its release from the ovary and the sperm after it enters the female genital tract is able to fertilize the ovum for generally not more than 48 hours". (1990: 139). He further clarifies that "if the menstrual cycles are regular and the woman is able to predict when the next period of bleeding would start, it would not be difficult to calculate the safe period. The situation is however, not so simple. There may be variation in the day of commencement and duration of menstrual bleeding. The number of days in different menstrual periods may vary. The day when the last bleeding episode commenced can, however, be readily recalled. The prediction of the day when next bleeding will commence is often difficult to predict. There are no firm and precise methods of calculation so to know the life span of sperms and ova". Thus, the rhythm method involves a number of technical aspects depending upon which a pregnancy can be made or avoided.

As mentioned above, conception takes place only when ovum and sperm are united in the female genital track during vulnerable period of conception. During this period, the couple may be united but ejaculation of semen outside the female genital tract may avoid a pregnancy. But this method is even not so safe to avoid a pregnancy. Technically lakhs of ovum are released during effective period and similarly the semen contains lakhs of sperms but only one sperm is fertilised with only one ovum. Thus, even if semen is ejaculated outside the genital tract to avoid a pregnancy during the vulnerable period of conception, slightest entry of semen or even entry of a single sperm into the said tract of the female spouse may cause pregnancy. Therefore, these methods have been found to be unsuitable in majority of cases. However, people of different regions adopt various other methods to reject a valid pregnancy—Raina notes that, "the abortificients taken by month reported, include papaya paste, turmeric power and mustard. There were reports of insertions of "a stick" with gree paste into the cervix, and use of some oral concoction" (1990: 138). In most of the tribal areas, people have also their indigenous devices and methods of family planning, for example among the Bonda tribe of Orissa, women take diluted saline water as oral drink or a combination of diluted saline water mixed with some roots and leaves of locally available plants. Similarly many other tribes have also their own indigenous means of avoiding pregnancy. But practically, as evidenced from laboratory tests, these have very little scientific efficacy of aborting a pregnancy. This has made a great concern for the Indian government as a result of which government has been popularising various modern and scientific birth control devices and their use among both the rural as well as urban people since 1960s. But nowadays more and more emphasis is being given on these methods as the pace of population growth in our country has become a matter of great concern for the whole world.

The modern family planning methods as available till date can broadly be divided into two parts, such as: (a) spacing method, and (b) terminal method. In a short, spacing method is a temporary and terminal method is a permanent way of family planning.

(A) Spacing Method

Spacing method is a temporary method of birth control measures by which a couple can maintain a regular space of time in between two birth depending upon one's own choice, desire or need. Thus, so long as a couple uses any of the devices available under these two category of methods, the female spouse is not conceived. The reverse effect is obtained simply by stopping the use of the device.

As available in government documents this method includes use of five contraceptives which provide effective protection against pregnancy; there are as follows:

(i) Condom

(ii) Diaphragm

(iii) Intra Uterine Devices (IUD)

(iv) Oral pills and

(v) Spermicides

Of these, condom is used by male spouses and the rest four contraceptives are used by female spouses. But any one of the above four contraceptives is used at a time by the female spouse for avoiding a pregnancy. And when a female spouse uses any of the said contraceptions the male spouse need not use of a condom. Hence use of any of the contraceptives by only one spouses makes a couple delaying a pregnancy or maintain a desirable gap between one child and the other. But each of these contraceptives has some merits and some drawbacks. However, the drawbacks are not observed in all cases as these vary from user to user depending upon its method of use and acceptability of the body of the user.

The uses, merits and drawbacks of the above contraceptives as mentioned by the Directorate of Advertising and Visual Publicity, Ministry of Information and Broadcasting, Government of India, 1991 (without page numbers) as mentioned below. However, in places the expressions have been technically simplified with additional information in order to make it lucid and understandable for the laymen.

(i) Condom

The condom is an extremity thin rubber sheet used by the male. It is unrolled on the erect male organ before having sex. As it covers the penis, the sperms cannot go into the women's body. While unrolling the condom on the male sex organ, a little space is to be left at the end so that the fluid after discharge can spill into it. A new condom is to be use every time so as to be avoid infection. At the end of each sexual act, the man must make sure to carefully withdrew his sex organ with the condom still in place to avoid spilling of semen into the vagina.

Merits

(a) It is the simplest and most effective method of avoiding pregnancy.

(b) There is no need to consult a doctor for using a condom.

(c) It protects against venereal diseases including the most dangerous disease, i.e. AIDS that has been frightful and alarming for the whole world.

(d) Its use can be discontinued without going to the family welfare centres or consulting any doctor or technical expert when a couple desires to have a child.

(e) It is readily available at all family planning centres free of cost and at a nominal price from the chemist, general stores, grocery and other shops even in remotest areas.

(f) There is no need of self restraint.

Drawbacks

In rare cases, an individual may be sensitive to rubber. A few men and women may find the rubber sheath an interference reducing the sexual sensation.

(ii) Diaphragm

The diaphragm is a rubber cap which is shaped like a dome with a spring in its ring. It is used by a women. She has to place it in her vagina before having sex so that it covers the opening to the womb.

It prevents pregnancy in a very simple way. The diaphragm blocks the opening of the womb with the result that the sperms cannot find their way towards the womb and thus no pregnancy takes place.

In order to make it most effective, it is better that some contraceptive jelly or spermidical cream is spread over the diaphragm before use. The cream would kill the sperms on contact.

To be practical, the diaphragm is to fit the vagina. As a result the women has to select the proper size of it with the help of a doctor who would also teach her how to fix and remove it so that later on she can do it herself without any problem.

Merits

(a) It does not interfere in the sexual act.

(b) It is a reversible and non-invasive method.

Drawbacks

(a) In rare cases an individual may be sensitive to rubber.

(b) The rate of failure can be quite high if not used properly.

(*c*) It needs elaborate preparation before the sexual intercourse which may not be possible every time.

(*d*) It has to be removed and washed each time after the sexual intercourse.

(*e*) High standard of hygiene is necessary in storage and use otherwise it can be a major source of infection.

(iii) Intra-Uterine Devices

'Intra-uterine' means inside the uterus and hence these are the devices which are placed in the womb for avoiding a pregnancy. There are many types of intra-uterine devices (IUDs). But in India, Lippes Loop and the Copper-T are most popular and hence commonly used among a large number of women.

Lippes Loop

The Lippes Loop is a small double 'S' shaped flexible device of fine plastic; about one and a half inch in length. The doctor or the trained nurse gently places this devices in the women's womb through her birth canal. No pregnancy occurs so long as the devices is present inside this canal.

Copper-T

Copper-T is also made of plastic but is wrapped with fine copper which enhances its contraceptive effect. Its acceptance is higher than loop. To secure highest contraceptive effect, the copper-T should be replaced every three years. The loop can, however, remain in place for several years without losing its contraceptive effect.

Merits

(*a*) Use of this device does not interfere with the sexual intercourse as its presence is not felt.

(*b*) Its insertion does not require hospitalisation.

(*c*) It is a reversible method and can be easily removed when a couple desires to have a child.

(*d*) The rate of failure of efficacy of this device is almost nil.

Drawbacks

(a) Side-effects, like heavier bleeding, backache and abdominal cramps may arise. Thee complains, however, invariably disappear after a few days or weeks.

(b) Adoption of this method is not suitable for delaying the first pregnancy.

(c) Sometimes the device is automatically expelled.

(iv) Oral Pills

Oral contraceptive pill is taken daily by mouth. If taken regularly as per the advice of the doctor, it provides almost 100 per cent protection against pregnancy. It works by suppressing the release of the egg cells by the ovaries. As no egg is released, pregnancy does not take place.

The pill is available in a pack of 28 tablets. One pill is taken daily beginning from 5th day of the onset of menstruation. The first 21 white tablets are contraceptive pills and the remaining 7 orange coloured pills and placebos. It is advisable that an extra pack is always kept handy, so that the next cycle can be started without brake. This regularity is the most important aspect which ensures the high efficacy of the method. However, if a pill is missed on a particular day the missed tablet should be taken as soon as possible, i.e. two tablets the next day; one in the morning and another in the evening. If missed on more than couple of occasions it should not be discontinued but another method of contraception such as condom should be used alongside upto the date of next menstruation cycle. However, the pill is prescribed by the doctor after examination of a woman by a doctor or trained nurse with the help of a check list. The pill should not be taken in case of the following situations:

(i) if the woman is pregnant,

(ii) if the woman is over 35 years of age,

(iii) if the woman has diabetes or there is a history of diabetes in her family,

(iv) if the woman had jaundice during the last six months,

(v) if the woman has cancer of the breast or genital organs,

(vi) if the woman is a nursing mother,

(vii) if the woman is suffering from high blood pressure, heart disease or rheumatism, and

(viii) if the woman is a smoker.

Generally oral pills are available in two different packs as Mala-N and Mala-D. The Mala-N packs are available in all the family welfare centres, hospitals or public health centres free of cost. But the Mala-D packs are available in the market in cheap rate. Apart from these two type of oral pill packets there are a number of other bands, such as: Pearl, Ecroz, Sukhi, Choice, Suvida, Moti, Apsara, Novelon, Triguilar, etc. which are available in the market. Apart from these, a weekly non-steroidal oral contraceptive like Saheli and Centron are also available in the market since 1st December, 1995 (Gol 401, 1996-97: 24).

Merits

(a) It is a reversible method of planning family.

(b) If taken regularly, it is 100 per cent effective.

(c) It is not coitus related, so there is no interference.

(d) It corrects pre-existing menstrual problems or irregular cycles.

(e) Because of regular check-up, most women have their breasts examined and crevical smears done frequently and any disease can get detected easily. It gives the women complete control over the situation and is particularly appropriate and safe for the use of young women below the age of 35.

Drawbacks

(a) As the pills acts by blocking the release of the eggs, it can simulate in some women the same symptoms as felt in early pregnancy. This is more so in the initial start-up period.

(b) Complaints, like dizziness, weight gain, vomiting, sickness or tenderness of breasts may occur. But all these disappear in 3-4 months of time.

(c) Sometimes irregular vaginal bleeding may occur.

(v) Spermicides

Literally spermicides mean the (chemical) agents that kill sperms. For this purpose, generally two types of agents are available in the market which are popular and widely accepted by a majority of women. These are: foam tablets and jelly cream. Hence, these are introduced in the vagina only 15 minutes before the intercourse.

The foam tablet that a woman inserts in her birth canal before having sex, produce some foam which protective coating to the whole area. It kills the sperms when come in contact with and thus it prevents pregnancy. The spermicidal cream is, similarly applied in the vagina with the help of an applicator. Like foam tablets, it also kills sperms on contact in the vaginal tract.

Merits

These tablets or creams are very effective. But their efficacy improves when used along with a diaphragm or condom in order to avoid any risk.

Drawbacks

(a) Being coitus-related procedures, it may be cumbersome to apply for some couples.

(b) It can be ineffective if used in small quantity or if they are not of good quality.

(c) After about one hour of its application it becomes ineffective. So, if intercourse takes place after this time, there may be risk of pregnancy.

(B) Terminal Methods

Terminal methods are permanent methods against pregnancy. Therefore, once the desired number of children are obtained one should adopt this method whereby, the couple would enjoy married life without any further fear of pregnancy whatsoever. Either the male spouse can undergo a simple operation for sterilization. Thus, by this method, risks of pregnancy is permanently avoided through sterilization process.

(i) Vasectomy

Sterilization of the male spouse is called vasectomy. It is a very simple outpatient procedure which takes hardly about 15-20 minutes of time. This operation involves a small cut, equal to the size as a grain of wheat above the man's scrotum on both the sides, i.e. on each side, a small portion of the vas or the tube which carries the seeds (sperms) is removed and the cut ends are tied up. The man's sex glands are not touched. He continues to enjoy sex as before. He also continues to ejaculate during sex but now his semen does not contain sperms or those seeds which cause pregnancy. There is no difference whatsoever in his strength or virility.

The man can return home, immediately after the operation is over. However, he should refrain from any strenuous manual labour or cycling for about one week. There is no other inconvenience. He can resume other normal works immediately. Further, it is necessary to use condom or any other contraceptive for about 15 ejaculations after the operation or abstain from intercourse for atleast three months. After the lapse of this period, the semen should be tested in the laboratory and if no sperms are found, there is no need of using any contraceptive in future.

Merits

(a) It is a simple operation.

(b) Its effectiveness against pregnancy is 100 per cent.

(c) It gives life long protection against unwanted pregnancies.

(d) There is no side-effect or complication.

Drawbacks

It is an irreversible method. In some cases, surgical recannalisation has been successfully, but the method is accepted as irreversible.

(ii) Tubectomy

Sterilization of female spouse is called tubectomy. In this operation, a small piece from each egg-tube (fallopian tube) of the woman are tied up the cut ends so as to block the passage of the egg cells. This way it cannot meet the sperm of the male seeds during intercourse and thus no pregnancy takes place. Tubectomy is done both by abdominal and vaginal routes.

In this case the woman has to remain for 2-3 in the hospital and needs to take complete rest for some days.

Merits

(a) Like vasectomy, it is also a permanent method of birth control measure.

(b) No side effect or complication occurs. However, this operation must be done by a competent doctor.

Drawbacks

It is an irreversible method and as such the couple cannot give a second thought for having a child after undergoing this operation.

So far as the couples effectively protected in India under the above method is concerned, the effectiveness is taken to be 100 per cent in case of sterilization, 95 per cent in case of IUD and 50 per cent in case of conventional contraçeptives" (GoI. 1998: viii).

CHAPTER–VI

SOCIETY, FAMILY AND FAMILY PLANNING

In this chapter, we have vividly discussed about the nature of society studied, rules of residence, family forms, notion of obtaining parenthood, desire of sex preference in birth, attitude towards family planning, adoption of family planning devices and other related aspects etc. as all these aspects are interrelated with one another and each one has its own significance on family planning and adoption of modern birth control measures for limiting one's family size.

Nature of Society and Rules of Residence

As mentioned in the introductory chapter, the main thrust of this piece of research surrounds four communities selected purposively from different social strata of Indian social order. This was done with a view to finding out the cross-cultural variations, if there are any. However, basing on the theoretical base we have selected Brahman (priestly class) from the upper most position of the Hindu social order, Chasa (agriculturist) from the middle social order and Bauri (an ex-untouchable community who now work as agricultural labourers) and Santal a tribal community (forest dwelling people who have migrated to Bhubaneswar city and earn livelihood as mainly construction workers and wage earners) from the lower social order. A total number of 50 households from each of these three ethic communities have been selected as sample for this study and the result is based on the members, particularly the household heads and their spouses belonging to these households.

The nature of society is highly influenced by family forms. Therefore, we may discuss the nature and social characteristics of the simple ethnic communities basing on the authority and descent system, residence of female spouses after marriage and acquisition of surnames by the male and female spouses and the legitimate children born to them after marriage.

All the four communities, viz Brahman, Chasa, Bauri and Santal are patriarchal, patrilineal and patrilocal in nature. As a result of this, all these communities are also patronymic by which a female spouse has to inherit the surname of her husband and the legitimate children born to her are also required to inherit the surname of their father (Table 6.1).

All the households of each community being patriarchal in nature, consider and recognise the senior male as the supreme authority of the household and hence the male family or household head enjoys exclusive power in the family or household as the case may be. He controls all the family members and family affairs. As patriarchal societies are also patrilineal in nature, the household head also inherits, controls and manages the whole of immovable as well as movable properties. All the family members are considered as subordinates to him and all of them are required to respect and obey him and respect his wishes, otherwise he may initiate action against the deviants as he deems fit. However, as in all the patriarchal households the eldest male or the father acts as the head and guardian, in matriarchal households the eldest woman or the mother acts as the head and guardian and thus all the members including the young men over women in patriarchal societies, where the women are considered as an underclass and hence, they are not consulted in any important familial matter and hence they are kept aside.

Patriarchal societies are patrilineal in descent order by which ancestry of the family is traced through the male line and the names upto certain past generations are propitiated and the annual *sradha* or oblation ritual is observed. In these societies the women ancestors are not considered as important as men ancestors. However, the female ancestors are offered annual oblations by their living male descendants in these societies. On the contrary in matriarchal societies more or less a reverse trend is observed.

In patrilocal societies, the female spouse has to leave her natal residence and comes to reside with her husband permanently at the latter's house. On the other hand, in matrilocal societies, after marriage, the male spouse has to leave his kith and kins and resides with her wife permanently at his affine's house as amongst the Khasis, Garos and Jaintias of Meghalaya.

Thus, since all the studied ethnic communities are patriarchal, patrilineal, patrilocal and patronymic in nature, women, in these communities do not find equal status with their male counterparts and as such, they are not consulted and their opinion is not normally recognised in important family affairs. They are provided with less opportunities for getting higher education and thus in these communities they remain as a subordinate class. However, even tough, like the Brahman, Chasa and Bauri Communities, the nature of Santal community is patriarchal, patrilineal, patrilocal and patronymic, women of this community enjoy more freedom as compared to women of the above communities, as because they are more or less economically independent and have higher earning capacity and thus they can desert their husbands if there is any intolerable compatibility.

Notion of Marriage and Attainment of Parenthood

Marriage is an important event in one's life. As a social institution marriage has various biological, social, ritual, psychological, economic as well as religious functions and implications. Therefore, in this regard marriage is a very essential socio-cultural institution in the part of a human being. However, the most important aspect and function of marriage is satisfaction of biological needs, i.e. fulfilling of sexual desire in a regularised manner and becoming parents through procreation of legitimate offsprings. Procreating of such offsprings through marriage is considered as the fulfillment of the psychological instinct and desire of becoming a recognised parent in the society.

The social status of a person, be a male or female, suddenly changes after his/her marriage, and his/her ritual/religious status also changes accordingly and hence he/she can perform certain social and ritual duties for his/her house or for the community as well. Thus, if a person does not get married and remains as unmarried for while of his/her life then he/she is not respected and ritually valued in the household as well as in the community concerned. Moreover, this social institution has another important function, this is, economic. Marriage leads to the establishment of household, and through it economic and social security of the family members is ensured.

In the above context, it was intended to know about the notion and perception of marriage and a question, like: "Is it necessary that a person should get married", was put to the informants. Interestingly each one of them irrespective of caste/community and sex replied that it is very essential (Table-6.2.1) and when a subsequent question relating to the factors for this was put as many as 12 reasons were put forth by the respondents (Table 6.2.2). Most of the male and female spouses of each community opined that this is the go the human society. Human beings are social beings and as such they live in society and they are to follow the societal norms. Therefore, it is essential for one and all they should get married. This view was expressed by 86 per cent of Brahman female spouses as against 84 per cent of Chasa, 68 per cent of Santal and 66 per cent of Bauri female spouses. So far as the case of the male spouses is concerned, 76 per cent of Brahman as against 74 per cent of Santal, 42 per cent of Bauri and 26 per cent of Chasa agreed with this opinion. Irrespective of community and sex, of the total 400 sample, 65.25 per cent are also of this opinion. The other reasons of getting married in descending order are: retention of *vamsa* (lineage) through procreation of children (21.75%), attainment of parenthood (17.00%), ensurement of livelihood through children (11.5%), fulfilment of biological needs, i.e. fulfilment sexual desire (11.00%), social/old-age security (9.5%), ritual/religious requirement (6.25%), sacrament through *mukhagni* (lightening of funeral pyre) and *pindadana* (offering of oblations) by male children (5.25%), protection of chastity (1.75%), generation of social responsibility among the youth (0.5%), essentially of *Grihasthashrama* (0.5%) and sharing of personal matters with a close relative, i.e., a life partner (0.25%).

These facts have been arranged in descending order of statistical importance. But practically, 'biological need' is the most important factor for marriage. In this context even though only 4 Santal male spouses and few Chasa and Brahman male spouses have opined that marriage is very essential for protection of chastity of girls, this factor seems to be very relevant. They have specifically said that if a person does not get married, there would be a lot of social problems. The important and foremost problem would be that the girls would become lecherous and the boys would become wayward and hence they would not concentrate in household works during their youth. This would certainly break down the whole social system.

Data available in the said table reveal some other facts too. One can observe that the Brahman people are traditionally religious minded and therefore, these people have specified various ideological and ritual factors of marriage like: sacrament of life after receiving mukhagni (funeral fire) and Pinda (annual oblations) from their own progenies, preferably by the eldest son. Therefore, they have categorically pointed out that marriage is essential for procreation of male children who would undertake these ideological and ritual duties for the parents.

Attaining parenthood is an important factor that fulfils the psychological requirement of proving oneself as capable of producing a child and hence becoming a socially recognised parent. This factor has been pointed out by a good number of male and female spouses of each community. Similarly retention of *vamsa* and old age or social security are two important factors which have been pointed out by a majority of people.

Children are considered as economic assets, mainly among the economically poor communities, and families that are engaged, in wage earning or having subsistence economy. Therefore, a good number of male and female spouses of Santal and Bauri communities who are basically wage earners, have opined that marriage is essential for improving the quality of life by earning through children. The Chasa, who practise agriculture, are also of the same opinion. They opine that marriage is essential to procreate children who would help their parents in their agricultural work and hence their quality of life would improve. However, as we have witnessed, a number of multifaceted answers have come out into the fore as the factors responsible for marriage, and there are good number of people who have justified procreation of children as one of the reasons among the 12 specified reasons for the marriage. But to a question relating to whether a married couple should procreate children, all irrespective of sex and community have pointed out that it is, of course, necessary that such of couple should procreate children (Table 6.3).

Notion of Sex Preference in Birth, the Girl Child and Family Planning

In a study on the 'Status of the Girl Child in Contemporary Societies', we have already discussed about the culture, notion of sex preference in birth verses the girl child. In this section we feel that part of analysis is also quite relevant here in the context of family planning. As traditionally in a patriarchal society the girl child has a subordinate status compared to a boy child, people prefer a boy child over a girl child. This compels many of them to go on procreating children until at least one boy child is born. This process certainly increases the family size of a person. However, it is worth quoting the section 'culture and the notion of sex preference in birth' discussed in the said study.

The social status of men and women differ from one society to another depending upon the nature of such societies. There are patriarchal and matriarchal societies; in the former type of societies the status of men is higher than that of women as in such societies the authority of the father or the eldest male member of the family is solely recognised and descent is traced through his line. Moreover, in this type of society the locality of residence of the female spouse changes after marriage to that of her husband's or any other affine and her surname is also changed according to the surname of her husband. The legitimate children born to her are also required to be known after the surname of her husband or the father of the children. As a matter of fact, in such societies, the male head remains as the absolute owner over all the ancestral properties and all such properties are inherited by the male children. Thus, in a patriarchal society women do not enjoy an equal status with their male counterparts in all respects; they are treated as subordinates or as underclass members in the family. And in most of the cases female children are considered as social and economic burden on the parents. What is more surprising is that, in this type of society, even a mother does not prefer a female child and if such a child is born to her she may not be very happy. This happens not because by nature she is biased or cruel towards female children rather she behaves negatively since she is socialised in such a society or culture. In this context an attempt has been made to find out the desired sex of the first child and further to ascertain the proportion of male and female children parents desire to beget among the four communities studied.

First of all a question relating to the 'desired sex' for their first issue was put, and most of them opined that they had desired for a boy child. Specifically highest per cent (94.00) of Bauris followed by 86 per cent of Santal, 84 per cent of Chasa and 76 per cent of Brahmans opined that they had wanted a male issue. Only 4 or 8 per cent of Brahmans and 1 or 2 per cent of Bauris said that they intended to have female issues. The rest in each community did not have any preference (Table 6.4).

The respondents who opined that they should have girl children adduced that betting first a girl child is an auspicious event and it is an indicator of prosperity for the family. But the respondents who had no option for any sex, opined that since formation of sex of a child is divinely ordained and humans cannot do anything to alter the sex of a child one should have no choice for a particular sex. If god wishes, it would give a male child otherwise a female one is begotten.

The respondents who had wanted male issues, pointed out as many as 6 multiple factors in order to justify their views. These factors are: (i) economic support to father, (ii) fulfilment of ritual requirement, (iii) social or old-age security, (iv) to continue family line or *vamasa*, (v) to remain free from dowry and marriage problems of daughters, (vi) to limit the family size. Of these factors, economic importance of male children is the most important reason behind opting for a boy child as in all the communities, most of the respondents, viz. 76.74 per cent of Santals, 72.34 per cent of Bauris, 71.05 per cent of Brahmans consider a male child as an economic asset. This, otherwise, means that these residents consider a girl child as an economic burden on them or their family. The next or second important factor is found to be social or old-age security which is thus: for Santals it is 23 or 53.49 per cent, for Bauris it is 21 or 44.68 per cent and for Chasas it is 13 or 30.95 per cent. But for the Brahmans the second most important factor comes to be the 'fulfilment of ascribed ritual duties since 19 or 50 per cent of informants of this community argued in its favour. However, if one looks at the data available in the total column, it is found that irrespective of any community, of the total 170 households who wanted male children, a total number of 124 or 72.94 per cent respondents pointed out economic importance of male children as the basic and foremost reason behind opting for a male child. The next important factor is observed to be social or old-age security of parents, as this factor has been focussed by a total number of 52 or 42.35 per cent or respondents. Old-age security of parents has been highlighted in the sense that either the male children or their spouses would be helpful to them during their old-age. Apart from them, the grandchildren would also equally be helpful to them during their old-age since as per the custom of the society girl children leave their parent's house after their marriage and permanently reside at the residence of their respective husbands. They visit their parents occasionally. Hence, a parent cannot demand the service of its married daughter during his/her old age. Another reason behind opting for male children is that the male children have many ritual duties to perform; as for example the eldest male child is required to offer some holy water of the *ganga* river in the mouth of his parents at the dieing moment and give *mukhagni* (lighting of funeral pyre) to their dead bodies, otherwise it is believed that the dead would not get *mukti* or mundane salvation. Hence, the souls of the dead (parents) would remain unsatisfied, and, therefore, their spirits might become malevolent and hence cause disturbances in the family. Next to this point, a total number of 33 or 19.41 per cent of respondents said that it is essential that one should have at least one male child in order to save and continue one's own agnatic line and hence inherit and protect the parental properties. Interestingly 10 or 5.58 per cent of respondents categorically stated a fact that it one gets a male child as its first issue, it would help the couple to limit the size of the family, otherwise the couple has to go in for procreating the next child with a hope to have a male issue. And if, the second issue is still a female one, the process of procreation does not stop until a male issue is begotten. This ultimately leads to creation of a large family and subsequently it becomes a great economic burden on the parents. So, if the first issue is a male child then it means, it would fulfil all the expected social ritual and economic obligations for the family. As a result one may stop procreation of more children after having a male child. (Table: 6.5).

Apart from asking about the desired sex of the first child, a subsequent question relating to gender discrimination, i.e. the total number of children a married couple should have and the sexual division thereof was put to the same informants in order to assess their temperament as regards gender biasness at the family level. The result of this question it presented in Table No. 6.6.1, 6.6.2, 6.6.3, 6.6.4, and 6.6.5.

Table No. 6.6.1 indicates that highest percentage of Santal, Brahman and Bauri respondents said that a couple should have at least 2 children, but out of the total of 50 sample respondents of each community, a total number of 35 or 70 per cent of Santal respondents favoured this; it is 24 or 48 per cent for the Brahman, and 14 or 28 per cent for the Bauri. A maximum of, that is, 19 or 38 per cent of Chasa respondents opine that a couple should have at least 3 children. However, the total figures reveal that out of the total respondents of all the four communities there are only 15 or 7.50 per cent of respondents who opine that a couple should have only one child as against 94 or 47 per cent of respondents who say that it should have a minimum 2 children.

The respondents who opt for 3 children per couple constitute 54 who comprise 27 per cent of the total sample size. Again quite a good number of households, i.e. 21 or 10.5 per cent are there who say that it should be 4 per couple and the respondents who want that a couple should have as many as 5, 6, 7 and 8 children, account for 1 or 0.5 per cent, 3 or 1.5 per cent, 2 or 1 per cent and 3 or 1.5 per cent respectively. The rest 7 or 3.5 per cent of respondents answered differently as they asserted that they are not sure about the number of children a couple should have since the number of children a couple gets is predetermined and man cannot do anything either to reduce or to increase the number. Absolutely it depends on the Almighty. If one interferes with this natural phenomenon through any artificial method the result may be detrimental.

Of the total number of respondents who preferred some definite number of children to have, the ratio of respondents wanted at least one boy child of the total desired number of children is found to be more than those who wanted at least one female child. However, among the Brahman respondents a total number of 48 or 96 per cent of respondents wanted at least one male child per couple as against the rest 2 (4.00%) respondents who did not have any choice of sex of their issues before they are born. Of the total 124 children wanted to have by the 50 sample households, the desired sex for 82 (66.13%) children was male and 39 (31.45%) children was female. For the rest 3 children the respondents did not have choice for any sex (Table 6.6.2).

Among the Chasas, Bauris and Santals, there are 46 or 97.87 per cent, 44 or 95.65 per cent and 48 or 96 per cent of respondents respectively who wanted that each of them should have at least one male child of the total number of children they desired. The respondents who wanted at least one girl child of the total number of children desired account, for 32 or 68.09 per cent for Chasa, 33 or 71.74 per cent for Bauri and 36 or 72 per cent for the Santal (Table 6.6.3, 6.6.4 and 6.6.5). However, the average number of male and female children opted to be begotten per couple shows an amazing fact. When in each of the communities, the average number of boy children wanted is 2 per family, it is less than 1 girl child per family.

Attitude towards Family Planning and Adoption of Modern Family Planning Methods

From the above dissuasion it is found that preference of male children over female children is a significant cause of enlargement of family size in patriarchal societies. However, in the contemporary societies, people conceptualise that one should not artificially limit the size of the family as it goes against the nature or will of the God. But at the present social scenario, human population has tremendously grown. But the natural as well as food resources are not increasing to cope up with the population growth. Therefore, there is stiff competition for easy survival. Still then there are many people who are tradition-bound and are not aware of the necessity of limiting their family size.

In the above context it was intended to know the opinion of the sample population about the necessity of limiting the family size. Interestingly of the total 200 male spouses, and 200 female spouses of all the four communities in total, as many as 155 or 77.5 per cent of male spouses as against 117 or 58.5 per cent of female spouses are of the opinion that there is necessity of limiting the family size and the rest go against this view (Table 6.7.1). A cursory look at the data available in the same table indicate that of the total male and female spouses of each sample community who are of the opinion that there is no need for planning to limit one's family size, comparatively more female spouses than the male ones are of this opinion. However, so far as the causes of planning for a small family size are concerned, the people who say that there is necessity for limiting family size, have focussed five interdependent factors (Table 6.7.2). These are: expectation to live happily (96.67%), getting better food (58.89%), providing better education to children (57.41%), providing better clothing for self and for children (48.89%) and remaining tension free (0.74%). To live happily is a broad concept which means to take enough and better food, to put on good clothes, to provide better education to children and to have a good house. If the income is less and the family size is large then there would be a number of persons to share the limited resources available and hence one would face a lot of problems. This is a stark materialistic statement. This factor has been pointed out by more than 85 per cent of respondents of each group. However, when more than 75 per cent of male and female spouses of each group have given stress on the fact that they would get sufficient and better food for themselves and also for their children if they have small family, there are only 30.23 per cent of female spouses as against 57.78 per cent of male spouses of Brahman community who have laid weightage on this point. On the contrary a reverse trend is seen in respect of this fact, that is, having a small family means it would enable the parents to provide better and higher education for their children. Comparatively there are quite high percentage of Brahman male (80.00%) and female (83.72%) spouses who have given stress on this aspect. Next to them there are the Chasas who have pointed out this too. The Brahmans are educationally as well as culturally more advanced than the rest 3 communities. Therefore, they do not like to deprive their children of development. They are very cautious about the 'intellectual property' of their family members which they would successfully achieve if they have smaller families. As these people are progressive than others among the sample groups, they also laid stress on the fact that they would be able to put on better dresses and provide the same to their children if they have smaller families. One important fact, pointed out by only 2 male spouses of Brahman community, that is, smaller family means living without tension, large family means inviting a number of problems and thereby tension and anxieties.

Now let us examine as to why the rest of the respondents have expressed their views negatively, that is, they should not plan to limit their family size. Some respondents have pointed out that one should not limit the family size through adoption of any modern family planning method. They have pointed out six factors to justify their views. All of them irrespective of sex and community have said that it is against the nature or will of the God. Children are the gift of God. So one cannot go against the divine will. If, at all, one goes against it, then he/she may face some mishaps. Next to this factor about 52 per cent of the respondents pointed out that more income is possible through the children. So if one has a number of children he/she can earn more through them and hence lead life happily. But when 76.19

per cent of Santal, followed by 63.64 per cent of Chasa and 37.5 per cent of Bauri men as against 74.42 per cent of Santal followed by 27.27 per cent of Bauri and 15.28 per cent of Chasa women said this, there is only one (20.00%) Brahman who is of this opinion. The Santal and Bauri respondents are mainly wage-earners who do not give any importance to education of their children rather engage them in various income generating and household duties from early childhood. They consider them as important economic assets and hence they claim that if one limits its family size then this goal would not be attained. Like these two communities, the Chasa respondents who traditionally earn their livelihood out of agriculture are also of this opinion. They say that they need more manpower to run their agricultural business. Surprisingly, as pointed out above, there is only one (20.00%) Brahman who has shared this opinion. This otherwise means that these people do not consider this factor as important as others do.

A total number of 12 to 9.23 per cent of respondents say that more children means more problems/sorrows, and less children means, happiness.

Next to this factor, there are 9 respondents, accounting for 6.92 per cent, who say that if one has more number of children, he/she is well protected and his/her paternal properties are well secured. If one has more number of children, particularly of male sex then the ancestral properties would be more safe.

There are 4 (80.00%) male and 3 (42.85%) female spouses in Brahman community who are of the opinion that it is non-heretic and hence is an offence against one's own religion (Table 6.7.3).

Current Adoption of Modern Family Planning Methods and Associated Factors

So far as current adoption of modern family planning methods is concerned of the total 50 potential couples of each community, there are as many as 21 or 42 per cent of Bauri couples who are now adopting some kind of family planning methods in order to reduce their family size. They are followed by 20 or 40 per cent of Brahman, 16 or 32 per cent of Chasa and 8 or 16 per cent of Santal couples who are also adopting this.

The rest of the couples are not adopting any family planning method (Table 6.8). So far as the awareness of family planning is concerned. Brahman couples are supposed to be more aware because of their education and hence more couples of this community should have adopted family planning methods. But practically it has not happened so, because of various reasons that we shall discuss later on.

Now let us discuss about the type of family planning methods adopted among the potential couples. Table No. 6.9.1 shows that out of the total 65 adopters among the sample communities, irrespective of sex as many as 49 or 75.30 per cent have undergone sterilization which is a permanent method of family planning. The rest 16 or 24.62 per cent, however, are now adopting other methods which are temporary in nature. So far as the community-wise adoption of sterilization method is concerned, out of the total of 16 Chasa and 8 Santal couples, as many as 14 or 87.50 per cent of Chasas and 7 or 87.50 per cent of Santals have undergone sterilization. They are followed by 17 or 80.95 per cent of the total 21 Bauris, and 11 or 55.00 per cent of the total 21 Bauris, and 11 or 55.00 per cent of the total 20 Brahman couples who have also undergone sterilization.

In Table No. 6.9.2, we have categorised the male and female sterilization cases. Interestingly, it is seen that of the total 49 couples who have undergone sterilization method, as many as 44 or 89.80 per cent of female spouses have undergone sterilization (tubectomy) and in the rest 5 or 10.20 per cent of cases men have undergone sterilization (vasectomy). The reasons for this are found to be several which we shall discuss later on.

If we analyse this phenomenon from a different angle, i.e. out of the total number of couples who are now adopting planning method and the percentage of different types of method, including male and female sterilization, a different picture comes into the fore. Irrespective of any community, of the total 65 couples adopting family planning methods, 67.69 per cent or 44 are the case of tubectomy. These cases are followed by 10.77 per cent or 7 couples who are using different types of oral contraceptive pills; 7.69 per cent or 5 couples who have adopted terminal methods, like using of copper T/or intra-uterine devices (IUD), and an equal percentage of couples have preferred male sterilization. Thus, the percentage of females sterilization to that of the total cases of sterilization is quite high. The couples who are now using condom account for only 4 or 6.15 per cent of the total adoptors of family planning methods. (Table 6.9.3).

As described in the earlier chapter, both male and female sterilization is a clinical process. Hence, the vasectomized or tubectomized persons are to go to the Family Health Care Centres or attend the locally organised camps or they are to go to any other such units, like hospitals, PHCs private clinics etc. where the facility is available for these methods. And the operated persons has to take a few days rest. Likewise a female spouse has to take the help of such a resource unit for taking copper T/IUD. Condoms of various brands are available in medical shops, stationary shops and even in betel shops. It is also supplied by the Government through Family Health Centres, PHCs, Hospital etc. free of cost. But the percentage of persons using this is less as because this method gives less sexual pleasure as reported. Likewise various types of contraceptive oral pill are also available in the market. The important brands as mentioned in Chapter-V are: Pearl, Ekroz, Subidha, Sukhi, Mala-D, Mala-N etc., and of these Mala-D and Mala-N are supplied by the Government free of cost. However, so far as community-wise adoption of individual methods is concerned, it can be said that of the total adoptors, majority have undergone tubectomy. But when 80.95 per cent or 17 Bauri couples have adopted this method, it is 75 per cent or 6 for the Santal, 68.75 per cent or 11 for the Chasa and 50 per cent or 10 for the Brahman couples. The percentage of adoption of this method is quite high among the Bauri, Santal and Chasa people as because the local ANMs play a major role in motivating these people to adopt this method. The ANMs motivate these people as they are illiterate and less exposed to the modern world of family planning, and hence, are easily motivated. The ANMs mainly target these people in order to achieve the target fixed by their authorities. The Brahmans are economically, educationally and culturally advanced and thus, have their own judgement in selecting a method of their choice. Therefore, use of oral pills (25.00%), Condom (10.00%), Copper-T/IUD (10.00%) is higher among the Brahmans than other communities (Table 6.9.3).

So far as the brands of oral pills used by the oral pill users is concerned, 3 or 60 per cent of the total 5 Brahman couples use Sukhi, and the rest 2 or 40 per cent use Pearl. These two brands of oral pills are available in the market and are considered as better than other pills. The only Chasa couple that uses oral pills is found to use Mala-D and the only Bauri couple that uses oral pills is found to take Mala-N. These two brands of oral pills are supplied by the government free of cost through the local PHCs and hospitals. And, as these people are poor, they prefer to use these pills. (Table 6.9.4).

Factors Responsible for Adoption of Tubectomy and Vasectomy

From the above discussion, it is learnt that comparatively very high percentage of female spouses have undergone sterilization. There are many factors responsible for this. They are either pressurised to undergo this operation or they voluntarily adopt this method. However, Table No. 6.10 indicates that of the total 6 Santal female spouses who have undergone sterilization, say that they have voluntarily adopted this method of operation, whereas out of the total 17 cases of the Bauri, 13 or 76.47 per cent have told that they voluntarily adopted this method. They are followed by 6 or 54.54 per cent of Chasa and 4 or 40 per cent of Brahman female spouses who have also voluntarily adopted this method of family planning. The rest say that they have adopted this method of family planning because of compulsion.

So far as the factors of undergoing tubectomy, pointed out by the female spouses are concerned, of the total 44 cases, as many as 34 or 77.27 per cent said that the male members or their husbands are the main bread-winner of the house. Hence they should always be physically fit to work. If a man undergoes family planning operation it would reduce his physical vigour and vitality and that would affect his working ability. Therefore, he should not undergo this operation. However, when 100 per cent Santals say this, it is 94.12 per cent of the Bauri, 72.73 per cent for the Chasa and 40 per cent of the Brahmans. Further, a total number of 12 or 27.27 per cent of female spouses have said that they have undergone sterilization as per the advice and psychological pressure of their male partners. But when there is not a single Santal female spouse who has said this, there are 4 (17.00%) Bauri, 4 (36.36%) Chasa, and 4 (40.00%) Brahman female spouses who have stated this. A total number of 3 or 50 per cent of Santal, 2 or 20.00 per cent of Brahman and 2 or 18.19 per cent of Chasa female spouses have categorically told that women are less labourious who just sit or can sit at home and eat, but men cannot do so. Therefore, they have undergone tubectomy operation. There is also another important factor that has been focussed by 6 or 13.64 per cent of sterilized women. They told that they had undergone this operation because of the pressure of their mothers-in-law who didn't allow their sons to get sterilized with a fear that they would lose their vigour, which would affect their bread-winning ability. (Table 6.11).

So far as the opinion of the husbands of operated women are concerned, out of the total 44 operated cases, 38 or 86.36 per cent said that they were always physically fit as they were to earn and feed the whole family. They did not undergo vasectomy operation because it would have put them in problems. They would not have been able to undertake hard labour which is an integral part of their daily chore. However, women attend to light domestic work, such as food processing and cooking, taking care of children and the sick and old members of the family. The husbands of all the 10 women of Brahman community, who have been tubectomized, are of this opinion as against the opinion of 7 or 63.64 per cent of Chasa, 3 or 50.00 per cent of Santal and 3 or 17.65 per cent of Bauri husbands. Those who are of the opinion that women are physically unfit to undertake hard work and hence are unable to earn for the whole family, account for 17 or 38.64 per cent of the total 44 cases (Table 6.12).

Knowledge and Sources of Information on Family Planning and Family Planning Methods

Regarding the knowledge on family planning and family planning methods it can be said that, all the eligible couples; both male and female spouses of each community, have knowledge on at-least on modern family planning method (Table 6.13). This has been possible mainly because of modernity, acculturation, and exposure to mass media, etc. which we shall discuss later on in this chapter. However, so far as the knowledge of the eligible couples on specific modern family planning methods is concerned, it is found that all the male and female spouses of each community have knowledge on both the male as well as female sterilization. But 65 per cent of either spouses say that they know about copper-T/Intra-Uterine Devices (IUDs). But when all the male and female spouses of the Brahman community know about this it is not so in case of other three communities. However, 95.5 per cent of female spouses as against 100 per cent of male spouses have knowledge about the use of condom. It is found that all except 9 or 18 per cent of Santal female spouses do not have any knowledge about it. Even if this method of family planning is comparatively less adopted among the rural people, the information about the use of this method has reached maximum number of people because of extensive exposure of them to various mass media. Use of oral pills is an important device but when all the male and female spouses of Brahman as well as Chasa community know about this method there are only 22 or 44 per cent of female spouses as against 16 or 32 per cent of Santal female spouses who seem to be knowledgeable about the use of this method. So far as the knowledge of male spouses of these two communities is concerned, there are 32 or 64 per cent of Bauri men and 21 or 42 per cent of Santal men who know about this (Table 6.14).

Source of knowledge is an important aspect of family planning. Nowadays, different government and non-government media play specific role in generating awareness on the necessity of limiting the family size through adoption of modern family planning methods. But people of all communities are not exposed to the same media. There are television, radio, newspapers, magazines, films, video screening etc. These media are normally available for the economically well-to-to and those whose awareness level is high. Hence depending upon this factor the awareness level of people differ.

Irrespective of communities, it is observed that the electronic media, like television and radio are two powerful agents that are considered as important mèdia for both men as well as women. But while television has played an important role in focussing the message of small family norm through adoption of various family planning methods for the Brahman and Chasa people, radio seems to be such as agent for the Bauri and Santal people. This is because the former two communities, are economically better off than the latter and hence they possess television which is a costly gadget as compared to the cost of a radio. On the other hand, the Bauris and Santals are mainly wage earners, and thus they possess radio, and most of them listen to it during their leisure time. However, the local ANMs are found to be important agents as the source of information on family planning for the Bauri and Santal women. In total, irrespective of communities 29 or 44.62 per cent of women as against 18 or 27.69 per cent of men say that they have come to know about the family planning method from the local ANMs and also the local doctors. The local ANMs have been the major source of information for these people as it is their duty to motivate the rural people for adopting modern family planning measures. The other sources of information for women include friends (30.46%), neighbours (21.54%), relatives (10.77%), own spouse (10.77%), PHCs/ hospitals (4.62%), newspapers/magazines (3.08%) and wall posters (11.5%). On the contrary, friends (69.23%), newspapers/ magazines (24.62%), PHCs/hospitals (13.85%), relatives (10.77%), posters (3.08%) and own spouse (1.54%) are the source of information for men (Table 6.15).

As mentioned above, the men are informed more by the newspapers than women as they are more exposed to this media. Similarly more men than women are found to have been knowledgeable about the family planning methods from the local PHCs/hospitals as they are more mobile and most frequently come to these places to avail medial facility for themselves as well as for their family members.

Post Operation Complications

Undergoing sterilization and post-operation complications are two important aspects of family planning in India. Most of the rural people are illiterate and have negative conception about the post-operation physical condition. The assume that occurrence of post-operation complications is a must. As they carry this conception in mind physically they remain vulnerable as if they would suffer from at least some complications when they undergo this operation. This leads them to consider any disease as the effect of this measure. However, out of the total 44 women and 5 men who have undergone sterilization, a total number of 26 or 59.09 per cent of women as against 2 or 33.33 per cent of men claim that they are suffering from various complications after they have undergone sterilization. When 81.82 per cent of Chasa, 58.82 per cent of Bauri, 50 per cent of Brahman and 33.33 per cent of Santal women claim that they are suffering from at least one post operation complications there are 33.33 per cent of Chasa men who say that they are also suffering from at least one ailment after sterilization. This only Santal man who has been sterilized is of the same opinion too (Table 6.16).

So far as the specific complications or diseases are concerned, irrespective of communities, of the total 26 women who suffer from post-operation complicacy, as many as 17 (65.33%) claim that they are suffering from headache and 12 or 46.15 per cent of women claim that they are also suffering from abdominal pain. The other important diseases from which these women are suffering include: waist pain (19.23%) joint pain (11.54%), dizziness (7.69%) and high blood pressure, gastric, nausea/vomiting and chest pain 3.85 per cent each. So far as the post operation complications of men is concerned, of the total 2 men who are suffering from post-operation problems, one claims that he is suffering from abdominal pain and hence unable to work hard. But both the men claim that they are suffering from dizziness. (Table 6.17).

Table—6.1: Nature of society according to ethnic groups (N = 50 For each caste)

Ethnic groups	*Authority*		*Lineage*		*Living place of female spouse after marriage*		*Inheritance of surname*	
	Patriarchal	*Matriarchal*	*Patrilineal*	*Matrilineal*	*Patrilocal*	*Matrilocal*	*Patronymic*	*Matronymic*
(1)	(2)	(3)	(4)	(5)	(6)	(7)	(8)	(9)
Brahman	50 (100.00)	–	50 (100.00)	–	50 (100.00)	–	50 (100.00)	–
Chasa	50 (100.00)	–	50 (100.00)	–	50 (100.00)	–	50 (100.00)	–
Bauri	50 (100.00)	–	50 (100.00)	–	50 (100.00)	–	50 (100.00)	–
Santal	50 (100.00)	–	50 (100.00)	–	50 (100.00)	–	50 (100.00)	–

Table—6.2.1: Is it necessary that a person should get married

Answers	*Brahman*		*Chasa*		*Bauri*		*Santal*	
	W	*H*	*W*	*H*	*W*	*H*	*W*	*H*
(1)	*(2)*	*(3)*	*(4)*	*(5)*	*(6)*	*(7)*	*(8)*	*(9)*
Yes	50 (100.00)	50 (100.00)	50 (100.00)	50 (100.00)	50 (100.00)	50 (100.00)	50 (100.00)	50 (100.00)
No	–	–	–	–	–	–	–	–

Note: (*i*) W = Wife, H = Husband

(*ii*) N = 50 for wife and 50 for husband of each group of population

(*iii*) Figures in brackets represent percentage.

Table—6.2.2: If yes, what are the factors responsible for this

Sl. No.	Factors	Brahman		Chasa		Bauri		Santal		Total		
		W N = 50	H N = 50	W N = 50	H N = 50	W N = 50	H N = 50	W N = 50	H N = 50	W N = 200	H N = 200	Both N = 400
(1)	(2)	(3)	(4)	(5)	(6)	(7)	(8)	(9)	(10)	(11)	(12)	(13)
1.	Ritual/religious requirement	2 (4.00)	17 (34.00)	–	4 (8.00)	–	2 (4.00)	–	–	2 (1.00)	23 (11.50)	25 (6.25)
2.	Sacrament through mukhagni and pinda dana by male children	1 (2.00)	15 (30.00)	–	5 (10.00)	–	–	–	–	1 (0.5)	20 (10.00)	21 (5.25)
3.	Grihastashrama is essential for salvation	–	2 (4.00)	–	–	–	–	–	–	–	2 (1.00)	2 (0.5)
4.	Go of the society/world	43 (86.00)	38 (76.00)	42 (84.00)	13 (26.00)	33 (66.00)	21 (42.00)	34 (68.00)	37 (74.00)	152 (76.00)	109 (54.50)	261 (65.25)
5.	Procreation of children/ retention of vamsa	9 (18.00)	12 (24.00)	8 (16.00)	18 (36.00)	9 (18.00)	6 (12.00)	18 (36.00)	7 (14.00)	44 (22.00)	43 (21.00)	87 (21.75).
6.	Old age/social security	5 (10.00)	5 (10.00)	8 (16.00)	5 (10.00)	4 (18.00)	6 (12.00)	2 (4.00)	3 (6.00)	19 (9.50)	19 (9.50)	38 (9.50)
7.	Biological need/ fulfilment of sexual desire	–	9 (18.00)	–	12 (24.00)	2 (4.00)	3 (6.00)	4 (8.00)	14 (28.00)	6 (3.00)	38 (19.00)	44 (11.00)
8.	Protection of chastity	–	1 (2.00)	–	2 (4.00)	–	–	–	4 (8.00)	–	7 (3.50)	7 (1.75)

(Contd...)

(1)	(2)	(3)	(4)	(5)	(6)	(7)	(8)	(9)	(10)	(11)	(12)	(13)
9.	To attain parenthood	6 (12.00)	18 (36.00)	13 (26.00)	8 (16.00)	13 (26.00)	3 (6.00)	3 (6.00)	4 (8.00)	35 (17.50)	33 (16.50)	68 (17.00)
10.	To earn livelihood through procreation of children	–	2 (4.00)	–	11 (22.00)	4 (8.00)	12 (24.00)	13 (26.00)	9 (8.00)	17 (8.50)	29 (14.50)	46 (11.5)
11.	Generation of social responsibility among the youth	–	2 (4.00)	–	–	–	–	–	–	–	2 (1.00)	2 (0.5)
12.	Sharing of personal matters with a close person; a life partner	–	1 (2.00)	–	–	–	–	–	–	–	1 (0.50)	1 (0.25)

Note: As per the Table No. 6.2.1.

Table—6.3: Is it necessary that a couple should procreate children after marriage

Answers	*Brahman*		*Chasa*		*Bauri*		*Santal*	
	W	H	W	H	W	H	W	H
(1)	(2)	(3)	(4)	(5)	(6)	(7)	(8)	(9)
Yes	50 (100.00)	50 (100.00)	50 (100.00)	50 (100.00)	50 (100.00)	50 (100.00)	50 (100.00)	50 (100.00)
No	–	–	–	–	–	–	–	–

Note: As per the Table no 6.2.1.

Table—6.4: Desired sex of the first child among different ethnic groups

Ethnic groups	*Boy child*	*Girl child*	*No option*	*Total*
(1)	*(2)*	*(3)*	*(4)*	*(5)*
Brahman	33 (76.00)	4 (8.00)	8 (16.00)	50 (100.00)
Chasa	42 (84.00)	–	8 (16.00)	50 (100.00)
Bauri	47 (94.00)	1 (2.00)	2 (4.00)	50 (100.00)
Santal	43 (86.00)	–	7 (14.00)	50 (100.00)
Total	170 (85.00)	5 (2.50)	25 (12.50)	200 (100.00)

Note: Figures in brackets represent percentage.

Table—6.5: Factors responsible for opting a boy child as the eldest progeny

Sl. No.	*Factors*	*Brahman*	*Chasa*	*Bauri*	*Santal*	*Total*
(1)	*(2)*	*(3)*	*(4)*	*(5)*	*(6)*	*(7)*
1.	Economic support to father	27 (71.05)	30 (71.43)	34 (72.34)	33 (76.74)	124 (72.94)
2.	Fulfilment of ritual requirement	19 (50.00)	7 (16.67)	6 (12.77)	5 (11.63)	37 (21.76)
3.	Old-age security	15 (39.47)	13 (30.95)	21 (44.68)	23 (53.49)	72 (42.35)
4.	To continue one's own vamsa	10 (26.32)	4 (9.52)	8 (17.02)	11 (25.58)	33 (19.41)
5.	To remain free from dowry and marriage problems of daughters	4 (10.53)	–	–	–	4 (2.25)
6.	To limit family	4 (10.53)	3 (7.14)	3 (6.38)	–	10 (5.88)

Note: Figures in brackets represent percentage.

Table—6.6.1: No. of children a couple should have

	No. of children									Total
Ethnic groups	*1*	*2*	*3*	*4*	*5*	*6*	*7*	*8*	*9*	
(1)	*(2)*	*(3)*	*(4)*	*(5)*	*(6)*	*(7)*	*(8)*	*(9)*	*(10)*	*(11)*
Brahman	3 (6.00)	24 (48.00)	19 (38.00)	4 (8.00)	–	–	–	–	–	50 (100.00)
Chasa	6 (12.00)	14 (28.00)	19 (38.00)	5 (10.00)	–	1 (2.00)	1 (2.00)	1 (2.00)	3 (6.00)	50 (100.00)
Bauri	3 (6.00)	21 (42.00)	8 (16.00)	9 (18.00)	1 (2.00)	2 (4.00)	–	2 (4.00)	4 (8.00)	50 (100.00)
Santal	3 (6.00)	35 (70.00)	8 (16.00)	3 (6.00)	–	–	1 (2.00)	–	–	50 (100.00)
Total	15 (7.50)	94 (47.00)	54 (27.00)	21 (10.50)	1 (0.50)	3 (1.50)	2 (1.00)	3 (1.50)	7 (3.50)	200 (100.00)

Note: Figures in brackets represent percentage.

Table—6.6.2: Option for boy and girl children among Brahman households

No. of children a couple should have	Total HHs opted	Total no. of children	No. of HHs opted for boy children	% age to total HHs opted	Total no. of boy children	% age to total children	No. of HHs opted for girl children	% age to total HHs opted	Total No. of girl children	% age to total children	HHs having no option for sex	% age to total HHs	Total children of any sex	% age to total children
(1)	(2)	(3)	(4)	(5)	(6)	(7)	(8)	(9)	(10)	(11)	(12)	(13)	(14)	(15)
1	3 (6.00)	3	2	66.67	2	66.67	–	–	–	–	1	33.33	1	33.33
2	24 (48.00)	48	23	95.83	30	62.5	16	66.67	16	33.33	1	4.17	2	4.17
3	19 (38.00)	57	19	100.00	39	68.42	16	84.21	18	31.58	–	–	–	–
4	4 (8.00)	16	4	100.00	11	68.67	4	100.00	5	31.25	–	–	–	–
Total		**124**	**48**	**96.00**	**82**	**66.13**	**36**	**72.00**	**39**	**31.45**	**2**	**4.00**	**3**	**2.42**

Note: Figures in brackets represent percentage.

Table—6.6.3: Option for boy and girl children among Chasa households

No. of children a couple should have	Total HHs opted	Total no. of children	No. of HHs opted for boy children	% age to total HHs opted	Total no. of boy children	% age to total children	No. of HHs opted for girl children	% age to total HHs opted	Total no. of girl children	% age to total children	HHs having no option for sex	% age to total HHs	Total children of any sex	% age to total children
(1)	(2)	(3)	(4)	(5)	(6)	(7)	(8)	(9)	(10)	(11)	(12)	(13)	(14)	(15)
1	6 (12.77)	6	6	100.00	6	100.00	–	–	–	–	–	–	–	–
2	14 (29.79)	28	13	92.86	15	53.57	10	71.43	10	35.71	1	7.14	2	7.14
3	19 (40.43)	57	19	100.00	42	73.68	14	73.68	16	28.07	–	–	–	–
4	5 (10.64)	20	5	100.00	12	60.00	5	100.00	8	40.00	–	–	–	–
5	–	–	–	–	–	–	–	–	–	–	–	–	–	–
6	1 (2.13)	6	1	100.00	4	66.67	1	100.00	2	33.33	–	–	–	–
7	1 (2.13)	7	1	100.00	6	85.71	1	100.00	1	14.29	–	–	–	–
8	1 (2.13)	8	1	100.00	7	87.50	1	100.00	1	12.5	–	–	–	–
Total	**47 (100.00)**	**132**	**46**	**97.87**	**92**	**69.70**	**32**	**68.09**	**38**	**28.79**	**1**	**2.13**	**2**	**1.52**

Note: (i) Figures in brackets represent % age.
(ii) 3 households out 50 sample household did not specified the no. of children a couple should have.

Table—6.6.4: Option for boy and girl children among Bauri households

No. of children a couple should have	Total HHs opted	Total no. of children	No. of HHs opted for boy children	% age to total HHs opted	Total no. of boy children	% age to total children	No. of HHs opted for girl children	% age to total HHs opted	Total no. of girl children	% age to total children	HHs having no option for sex	% age to total HHs	Total children of any sex	% age to total children
(1)	(2)	(3)	(4)	(5)	(6)	(7)	(8)	(9)	(10)	(11)	(12)	(13)	(14)	(15)
1	3 (6.52)	3	3	100.00	3	100.00	–	–	–	–	–	–	–	–
2	21 (45.65)	42	20	95.24	25	59.52	15	71.43	15	35.71	1	4.76	2	4.76
3	8 (17.39)	24	8	100.00	17	70.83	7	87.50	7	29.17	–	–	–	–
4	9 (19.57)	36	8	88.89	24	66.67	7	77.78	8	22.22	1	11.11	4	11.11
5	1 (2.17)	5	1	100.00	5	100.00	–	–	–	–	–	–	–	–
6	2 (4.35)	12	2	100.00	9	75.00	2	100.00	3	25.00	–	–	–	–
7	–	–	–	–	–	–	–	–	–	–	–	–	–	–
8	2 (4.35)	16	2	100.00	11	68.75	2	100.00	5	31.25	–	–	–	–
Total	**46 (100.00)**	**138**	**44**	**95.65**	**94**	**68.12**	**33**	**71.74**	**38**	**27.54**	**2**	**4.35**	**6**	**4.35**

Note: Figures in brackets represent % age.

Table—6.6.5: Option for boy and girl children among Santal households

No. of children a couple should have	*Total HHs opted*	*Total no. of children*	*No. of HHs opted for boy children*	*% age to total HHs opted*	*Total no. of boy children*	*% age to total children*	*No. of HHs opted for girl children*	*% age to total HHs opted*	*Total no. of girl children*	*% age to total children*	*HHs having no option for sex*	*% age to total HHs*	*Total children of any sex*	*% age to total children*
(1)	*(2)*	*(3)*	*(4)*	*(5)*	*(6)*	*(7)*	*(8)*	*(9)*	*(10)*	*(11)*	*(12)*	*(13)*	*(14)*	*(15)*
1	3 (6.00)	3	3	100.00	3	100.00	7	–	–	–	–	–	–	–
2	35 (70.00)	70	33	94.29	38	54.29	26	74.29	28	40.40	2	5.71	4	5.71
3	8 (16.00)	24	8	100.00	16	66.67	8	100.00	8	33.33	–	–	–	–
4	3 (6.00)	12	3	100.00	6	50.00	2	66.67	6	50.00	–	–	–	–
5	–	–	–	–	–	–	–	–	–	–	–	–	–	–
6	–	–	–	–	–	–	–	–	–	–	–	–	–	–
7	1 (2.00)	7	1	100.00	7	100.00	–	–	–	–	–	–	–	–
Total	**50 (100.00)**	**116**	**48**	**96.00**	**70**	**60.34**	**36**	**72.00**	**42**	**36.21**	**2**	**4.00**	**4**	**3.45**

Note: *(i)* The average in 'a' column has been worked out from those who opted boy or girl children and the average in 'b' column has been worked out from the total households.

(ii) Figures in brackets represent % age.

Table—6.7.1: Is there any necessity that a couple should plan (limit) its family size

Answer	*Brahman*		*Chasa*		*Bauri*		*Santal*		*Total*		
	W	*H*	*W*	*H*	*W*	*H*	*W*	*H*	*W* N = 200	*H* N = 200	*T* N = 400
(1)	*(2)*	*(3)*	*(4)*	*(5)*	*(6)*	*(7)*	*(8)*	*(9)*	*(10)*	*(11)*	*(12)*
Yes	43 (86.00)	45 (90.00)	37 (74.00)	39 (78.00)	28 (56.00)	42 (84.00)	7 (14.00)	29 (58.50)	117 (58.50)	155 (77.5)	272 (68.00)
No	7 (14.00)	5 (10.00)	13 (26.00)	11 (22.00)	22 (44.00)	8 (16.00)	43 (86.00)	21 (42.00)	83 (41.5)	45 (22.5)	128 (32.00)

Note: As per the Table No. 6.2.1.

Table—6.7.2: If yes, what are the reasons

Sl.	Reasons	Brahman		Chasa		Bauri		Santal		Total		
No.		W N = 43	H N = 45	W N = 37	H N = 39	W N = 28	H N = 42	W N = 7	H N = 29	W N = 115	H N = 115	T N = 270
(1)	(2)	(3)	(4)	(5)	(6)	(7)	(8)	(9)	(10)	(11)	(12)	(13)
1	To live well	40 (93.02)	45 (100.00)	37 (100.00)	37 (94.87)	24 (85.71)	42 (100.00)	7 (100.00)	29 (100.00)	108 (93.91)	153 (98.71)	261 (96.71)
2	It will enable parents to feed better	13 (30.23)	26 (57.78)	37 (100.00)	32 (82.05)	24 (85.71)	42 (100.00)	7 (100.00)	22 (75.86)	81 (70.43)	78 (50.32)	159 (58.89)
3	It will enable to provide better clothing to children	29 (67.44)	40 (88.89)	17 (45.95)	22 (56.41)	6 (21.43)	13 (30.95)	1 (14.29)	4 (13.79)	53 (46.09)	79 (50.97)	132 (48.89)
4	It will enable to provide better education to children	36 (83.72)	36 (80.00)	19 (51.35)	28 (71.79)	4 (14.29)	16 (38.1)	3 (42.86)	12 (41.38)	62 (53.91)	93 (60.0)	155 (57.41)
5	Small family has less problem/tension	–	2 (4.44)	–	–	–	–	–	–	–	2 (1.29)	(0.74)

Note: As per the Table No. 6.2.1.

Table—6.7.3: If no, what are the reasons

Sl. No.	Reasons	Brahman		Chasa		Bauri		Santal		Total		
		W (N = 7)	H (N = 5)	W (N = 13)	H (N = 11)	W (N = 22)	H (N = 81)	W (N = 43)	H (N = 21)	W (N = 85)	H (N = 45)	T (N = 130)
(1)	(2)	(3)	(4)	(5)	(6)	(7)	(8)	(9)	(10)	(11)	(12)	(13)
1	Non-religious	3 (42.85)	4 (80.00)	–	–	–	–	–	–	3 (3.5)	4 (8.89)	7 (5.38)
2	Against the will of the God	7 (100.00)	5 (100.00)	13 (100.00)	11 (100.00)	22 (100.00)	8 (100.00)	43 (100.00)	21 (100.00)	85 (100.00)	45 (100.00)	130 (100.00)
3	Better income through progenies	–	1 (20.00)	2 (15.38)	7 (63.64)	6 (27.27)	3 (37.5)	32 (74.42)	16 (76.19)	40 (47.65)	27 (60.00)	67 (51.54)
4	Self and family protection	–	3 (60.00)	1 (7.69)	3 (27.27)	–	2 (25.00)	–	–	1 (1.18)	81 (17.18)	9 (6.92)
5	Sharing of problems/ happiness	3 (42.85)	2 (40.00)	2 (15.38)	–	–	–	3 (6.98)	2 (9.52)	8 (9.41)	4 (8.89)	12 (9.23)
6	Afraid of adopting any family planning method	–	–	–	–	1 (4.55)	–	3 (6.98)	–	4 (4.7)	–	4 (3.08)

Note: As per Table No. 6.2.1.

Table—6.8: No. of couples presently adopting modern family planning measures

Variables	*Brahman (N = 50)*	*Chasa (N = 50)*	*Bauri (N = 50)*	*Santal (N = 50)*	*Total (N = 200)*
(1)	*(2)*	*(3)*	*(4)*	*(5)*	*(6)*
Adopting	20 (40.00)	16 (32.00)	21 (42.00)	8 (16.00)	65 (32.50)
Non adopting	30 (60.00)	34 (68.00)	29 (58.00)	72 (84.00)	135 (67.50)

Note: Figures in brackets represent percentage.

Table—6.9.1: Type of adoption of modern family planning measures among adoptors

	Brahman (N = 20)	*Chasa (N = 16)*	*Bauri (N = 21)*	*Santal (N = 8)*	*Total (N = 65)*
Sterilization	11 (55.00)	14 (87.50)	17 (80.95)	7 (87.50)	49 (75.38)
Others	9 (45.00)	2 (12.00)	4 (19.05)	1 (12.50)	16 (24.62)

Note: Figures in brackets represent percentage.

Table—6.9.2: Percentage of female and male sterilization among the total sterilized couples

Type of sterilization	*Brahman (N = 11)*	*Chasa (N = 14)*	*Bauri (N = 17)*	*Santal (N = 7)*	*Total (N = 49)*
Female sterilization	10 (90.91)	11 (78.57)	17 (100.00)	6 (85.71)	44 (89.80)
Male sterilization	1 (9.09)	3 (21.43)	–	1 (14.29)	5 (10.20)

Note: Figures in brackets represent percentage.

Table—6.9.3: Type of adoption of modern family planning measures among adoptors

	Brahman (N = 20)	Chasa (N = 16)	Bauri (N = 21)	Santal (N = 8)	Total (N = 65)
(1)	(2)	(3)	(4)	(5)	(6)
Tubectomy	10 (50.00)	11 (68.75)	17 (80.95)	6 (75.00)	44 (67.69)
Vasectomy	1 (5.00)	3 (18.75)	–	1 (12.50)	5 (7.69)
Copper T/ IUD	2 (10.00)	1 (6.25)	1 (4.76)	1 (12.50)	5 (7.69)
Condom	2 (10.00)	–	2 (9.52)	–	4 (6.15)
Oral pills	5 (25.00)	1 (6.25)	1 (4.76)	–	7 (10.77)

Note: Figures in brackets represent percentage.

Table—6.9.4: Name of oral pills used by the pill users

Name of pills	Brahman (N = 5)	Chasa (N = 1)	Bauri (N = 1)	Santal (N = 0)
(1)	(2)	(3)	(4)	(5)
Sukhi	3 (60.00)	–	–	–
Pearl	2 (40.00)	–	–	–
Mala-D	–	1 (100.00)	–	–
Mala-N	–	–	1 (100.00)	–

Note: Figures in brackets represent percentage.

Table—6.10: Willingness for undergoing tubectomy among sterilized wives

Variable	*Brahman (N = 10)*	*Chasa (N = 11)*	*Bauri (N = 17)*	*Santal (N = 6)*
(1)	*(2)*	*(3)*	*(4)*	*(5)*
Voluntarily	4 (40.0)	6 (54.55)	13 (76.47)	6 (100.00)
By force/ compulsion	6 (60.00)	5 (45.45)	4 (23.53)	–

Note: Figures in brackets represent percentage.

Table—6.11: Factors responsible for adopting tubectomy (opinion of sterilized wives)

Sl. No.	*Factors*	*Brahman (N = 10)*	*Chasa (N = 11)*	*Bauri (N = 17)*	*Santal (N = 6)*	*Total (N = 44)*
(1)	*(2)*	*(3)*	*(4)*	*(5)*	*(6)*	*(7)*
1	Husband should be physically fit to earn as he is the main bread earner	4 (40.00)	8 (72.73)	16 (94.12)	6 (100.00)	34 (77.27)
2	As per the advice force of husband	4 (40.00)	4 (36.36)	4 (23.53)	–	12 (27.27)
3.	As per the advice force of mother-in-law	2 (20.00)	4 (36.36)	–	–	6 (13.64)
4	Families are less laborious they can just sit and eat	2 (20.00)	2 (18.19)	–	3 (50.00)	7 (15.91)

Note: Figures in brackets represent percentage.

Table—6.12: Factors responsible for adpoting more tubectomy (opinion of husbands of sterilized wives)

Sl. No.	*Factors*	*Brahman (N = 10)*	*Chasa (N = 11)*	*Bauri (N = 17)*	*Santal (N = 6)*	*Total (N = 44)*
(1)	(2)	(3)	(4)	(5)	(6)	(7)
1	Husband should be physically fit to earn as he is the main bread earner	4 (40.00)	11 (100.00)	17 (100.00)	6 (100.00)	38 (86.36)
2	Female are physically unfit to do hand labour and earn for the whole family	4 (40.00)	7 (63.64)	3 (17.65)	3 (50.00)	17 (38.64)
3	Female can just sit and eat but males can not	10 (100.00)	7 (63.64)	3 (17.65)	3 (50.00)	23 (52.27)

Note: Figures in brackets represent percentage.

Table—6.13: Knowledge of all couples on at least one modern family planning method

Variables	*Brahman*		*Chasa*		*Bauri*		*Santal*		*Total*	
	W N = 50	H N = 50	W N = 50	H N = 50	W N = 50	H N = 50	W N = 50	H N = 50	W 200	H 200
(1)	*(2)*	*(3)*	*(4)*	*(5)*	*(6)*	*(7)*	*(8)*	*(9)*	*(10)*	*(11)*
Have	50 (100.00)	50 (100.00)	50 (100.00)	50 (100.00)	50 (100.00)	50 (100.00)	50 (100.00)	50 (100.00)	200 (100.00)	200 (100.00)
Do not have	–	–	–	–	–	–	–	–	–	–

Note: Figures in brackets represent percentage.

Table—6.14: Knowledge of all couples on specific modern family planning methods

Variable	*Brahman*		*Chasa*		*Bauri*		*Santal*		*Total*	
	W *N = 50*	*H* *N = 50*	*W* *N = 50*	*H* *N = 50*	*W* *N = 50*	*H* *N = 50*	*W* *N = 50*	*H* *N = 50*	*W* *200*	*H* *200*
(1)	*(2)*	*(3)*	*(4)*	*(5)*	*(6)*	*(7)*	*(8)*	*(9)*	*(10)*	*(11)*
Male sterilization	50 (100.00)	50 (100.00)	50 (100.00)	50 (100.00)	50 (100.00)	50 (100.00)	50 (100.00)	50 (100.00)	200 (100.00)	200 (100.00)
Female sterilization	50 (100.00)	50 (100.00)	50 (100.00)	50 (100.00)	50 (100.00)	50 (100.00)	50 (100.00)	50 (100.00)	200 (100.00)	200 (100.00)
Copper-T/IUD	50 (100.00)	50 (100.00)	33 (66.00)	40 (80.00)	30 (60.00)	28 (56.00)	17 (34.00)	12 (24.00)	130 (65.00)	130 (65.00)
Condom	50 (100.00)	50 (100.00)	50 (100.00)	50 (100.00)	50 (100.00)	50 (100.00)	41 (82.00)	50 (100.00)	191 (95.5)	200 (100.00)
Oral pills	50 (100.00)	50 (100.00)	50 (100.00)	50 (100.00)	22 (44.00)	32 (64.00)	16 (32.00)	21 (42.00)	138 (69.00)	153 (76.50)
Others methods	–	2 (4.00)	–	–	–	–	–	–	–	2 (1.00)

Note: Figures in brackets represent percentage.

Table—6.15: Sources of knowledge among family planning adoptors

Sl. No.	Sources of knowledge	*Brahman* N = 20		*Chasa* N = 16		*Bauri* N = 21		*Santal* N = 8		*Total* N = 65	
		W	H	W	H	W	H	W	H	W	H
(1)	(2)	(3)	(4)	(5)	(6)	(7)	(8)	(9)	(10)	(11)	(12)
1	Television	14 (70.00)	20 (100.00)	6 (37.5)	16 (100.00)	6 (28.57)	14 (66.67)	2 (25.00)	3 (37.5)	28 (43.08)	53 (81.54)
2	Radio	6 (30.00)	3 (15.00)	6 (37.5)	7 (43.75)	10 (47.62)	13 (61.90)	4 (50.00)	4 (50.00)	26 (40.00)	27 (41.54)
3	ANM/Doctor	2 (101.00)	3 (15.00)	7 (43.75)	4 (25.00)	17 (80.95)	6 (38.10)	3 (37.5)	3 (37.5)	29 (44.62)	18 (27.69)
4	Poster	1 (5.00)	–	–	–	–	1 (4.76)	–	1 (12.5)	1 (1.5)	2 (3.08)
5	PHC/Hospital	3 (15.00)	–	–	4 (25.00)	–	4 (19.05)	–	1 (12.5)	3 (4.62)	9 (13.85)
6	Friends	4 (26.00)	18 (90.00)	6 (37.5)	10 (62.5)	14 (66.67)	16 (76.19)	1 (12.5)	1 (12.5)	25 (38.46)	45 (69.23)
7	Relatives other than spouses	2 (10.00)	–	3 (18.75)	7 (43.75)	–	–	2 (25.00)	–	7 (10.77)	7 (10.77)
8	Neighbour	–	–	6 (37.5)	–	6 (28.57)	–	2 (25.00)	–	14 (21.54)	–
9	News paper/ magazines	2 (10.00)	9 (45.00)	–	6 (37.5)	–	–	–	1 (12.5)	2 (3.08)	16 (24.62)
10	Spouse	3 (15.00)	–	7 (43.75)	–	–	1 (4.76)	–	–	7 (10.77)	1 (1.54)

Note: Figures in brackets represent percentage.

Table—6.16: Post operation problems, complications among the sterilized spouses

Variables	*Brahman*		*Chasa*		*Bauri*		*Santal*		*Total*	
	W N = 10	*H* N = 1	*W* N = 11	*H* N = 3	*W* N = 17	*H* N = 0	*W* N = 6	*H* N = 6	*W* 44	*H* 5
(1)	*(2)*	*(3)*	*(4)*	*(5)*	*(6)*	*(7)*	*(8)*	*(9)*	*(10)*	*(11)*
No problems	5 (50.00)	1 (100.00)	2 (18.18)	2 (66.67)	7 (41.18)	–	6 (66.67)	–	18 (40.91)	3 (66.67)
Having problems	5 (50.00)	–	9 (81.82)	1 (33.33)	10 (58.82)	–	22 (33.33)	1 (100.00)	26 (59.09)	2 (33.00)

Note: Figures in brackets represent percentage.

Table—6.17: Post operation problems among sterilized couples

Sl. No.	Types of problems	Brahman		Chasa		Bauri		Santal		Total	
		W N = 5	H N = 0	W N = 9	H N = 1	W N = 10	H N = 0	W N = 2	H N = 1	W N = 26	H N = 2
(1)	(2)	(3)	(4)	(5)	(6)	(7)	(8)	(9)	(10)	(11)	(12)
1	Abdominal pain	2 (40.00)	–	5 (55.56)	–	5 (50.00)	–	–	1 (50.00)	12 (46.15)	1 (50.00)
2	Waist pain	2 (40.00)	–	1 (11.11)	–	–	–	2 (100.00)	–	5 (19.23)	–
3	Headache	1 (20.00)	–	7 (77.78)	–	8 (80.00)	–	1 (50.00)	–	17 (65.38)	–
4	Dizziness	1 (20.00)	–	1 (11.11)	1 (100.00)	–	–	–	–	2 (7.69)	2 (50.00)
5	Joint pain	–	–	–	–	2 (20.00)	–	1 (50.00)	–	3 (11.54)	–
6	High BP	–	–	1 (11.11)	–	–	–	–	–	1 (3.85)	–
7	Gastric	–	–	–	–	1 (10.00)	–	–	–	1 (3.85)	–
8	Delayed healing	1 (20.00)	–	–	–	–	–	–	–	1 (3.85)	–
9	Nausea/vomiting	–	–	–	–	1 (10.00)	–	–	–	1 (3.85)	–
10	Chest pain	–	–	–	–	1 (10.00)	–	–	–	1 (3.85)	–

Note: Figures in brackets represent percentage.

CHAPTER—VII

Government Schemes and Facilities on Family Planning and Level of Awareness

Green Card Facility

In order to reduce the decennial growth rate, government has formulated various schemes and facilities for the eligible couples who adopt permanent family planning method. The most important scheme is 'Green Card' facility. The facilities under this scheme are many. As per the Resolution No. 34707H, dated 19.10.83 and subsequent orders issued in that connection, the couples, having one or two children, who accept terminal (tubectomy/vasectomy) method of contraception, are entitled to the benefits enunciated by the Health and Family Welfare Department. The concise benefits to which a 'Green Card' holder is entitled from the date of its operation are as follows:

1. Preference is given to them in allotment of houses constructed by government or Housing Board in urban and rural areas by reserving 5 per cent of such houses.

2. Homestead land measuring 8 decimals is given to such families free of premium as against 4 decimals now being provided to the persons having no such land.

3. Preference is given to these families in providing LIG and MIG housing loan by reserving 5 per cent of the total amount.

4. Reservation of 5 per cent seats in engineering, medical, polytechnic and I.T.I. institutions is made for the admission of children of these families.

5. In case the card holder happens to be a state government employee, he or she is to get an incentive allowance equivalent to twice the amount of his annual increment.

6. And under the 'Green Card Scheme', a special lottery programme would be introduced for the 'Green Card' holders. The lottery would be instituted in each of the 314 blocks and 36 Municipalities/N.A.Cs and would carry a prize of Rs. 10,000.00 each. Each 'Green Card' holder would be entitled to participate in the lottery for 5 draws including the one to be held during the year in which he/she was sterilized. Once he/she gets a prize, he/she will not be entitled to participate in subsequent draws. (Go0, undated: 2).

In a valuable document, that is the Government Resolution, No. F.W. IG-3/81 (P+ 111), 42057/H, dt. 30.11.83, it is mentioned that the following facts which an operated person should know:

(a) the 'Green Card' should be treated as a valuable document and carefully preserved.

(b) This should not be handed over to anyone else for use.

(c) The card holder may apply to the concerned authorities giving card number and attested copy of the certificate of Director of Family Welfare in order to get benefit laid down in the resolution. The original card should not be handed over on any account. It can only be shown to the officer concerned for granting the benefit.

(d) If the card is lost/damaged, the card holder may have to apply to the Director, Family Welfare for a duplicate copy through the medical officer of the concerned P.H.C. in the prescribed form after depositing Rs. 10/- as application fee.

(e) Entitlements of Green Card holders have been recorded at page-6 of the Green Card. As soon as any of the benefits is given to the card holder, the same shall be entered in the appropriate place at page-10-12 of the card with dated signature and seal of the officer concerned.

(f) The officer from the Directorate/Districts going on tour to different P.H.C.s shall check up the Green Card Registers maintained in the P.H.C.s and indicate the same in their tour diaries.

(g) And this may be brought to the notice of all concerned (ibid. p. 3-4).

Thus, the above facts show that the government is seriously concerned about the operation of Green Card Scheme and how effectively the card holders would get the benefits made available by the government. However, maternity leave is sanctioned to a woman employee only for the first and second issues, and from 17th August, 1984 it has been decided by the government not to sanction maternity leave to a woman government servant for her third and subsequent issues. This rule has been enforced with a view to popularize the concern of the state regarding the necessity of reducing family size.

Monthly financial benefit to the government servants adopting sterilization seems to be the most important and lucrative incentive that attracts an eligible government servant for adopting the said family planning method. In this regard, an Office Order (No. 05.346/84/22984/p) was issued on 4th June, 1985, from the Finance Department mentioning the detailed provisions of financial incentive equivalent to two increment of the concerned government servant. The order is as follows:

1. It appears that under Government of India service such benefit is allowed to an employee as personal pay, the quantum of which remains unchanged during the entire service career of the government servant concerned. The personal pay is neither taken into account at the time of fixation of pay of promotion of a government servant to the higher grade nor deducted on his reversion to the lower grade. This personal pay is treated is a sort of *'incentive allowance'*.

2. Keeping in view the procedure adopted by the Govt. of India in this regard, the state government has been pleased to pass an order that its employees in possession of 'Green Card; would be entitled to incentive allowances detailed below:

   (a) The incentive allowance would be equal to twice the amount of increment admissible to a government servant on the date he/she is declared eligible for this allowance and in case the government servant is on foreign service, on the eligible date the aforesaid increment admissible in his/her parent scale will be taken into account.

   (b) The benefit of incentive allowance would be allowed even if an employee is held up at the efficiency bar stage of his/her time scale.

   (c) The incentive allowance is not to be taken into account for fixation of pay on promotion and the benefit of incentive allowance would continue to be available at the same rate even after promotion.

   (d) Once the employee gets the benefit of incentive allowance at a particular rate, he would continue to draw the same even if he is reduced to a lower stage in his time scale of pay or reduced to lower scale/grade or post by way of penalty under the provisions of O.C.S. (classification, control and appeal) Rules, 1992.

(e) If the 'Green Card' holder was entitled to the benefit of the incentive allowance before his suspension as a disciplinary measure he would continue to get the incentive allowance at the rate allowed to him over and above the subsistence allowance admissible but if he becomes entitled to, during the period of suspension the said allowance would be drawn only after suspension.

(f) If a 'Green Card' holder was entitled to incentive allowance before proceeding on leave, incentive allowance would be admissible to him during the period of leave over and above leave salary. However, in case, a government servant possesses Green Card during the period of leave incentive allowance would be admissible to him with effect from the date he resumes duty after availing leave.

(g) If a government servant possesses a 'Green Card' during the period of training for which he is deputed in public interest and the training is treated as duty, he would be entitled to incentive allowance during the period of training.

(h) This incentive allowance would be admissible over and above other cash incentive, if any received by the 'Green Card' holder.

(i) Whether both husband and wife are Government servants, incentive allowance may be drawn by either of them on production of 'Green Card'.

(j) The benefit of incentive allowance would be sanctioned from 1st day of the month following the date of sterilization after 19.10.1983 i.e., the date of issue of the resolution No. 34707/dt. 19.10.1983 of Health and Family Welfare Department.

(k) And incentive allowance would be sanctioned by the authority competent to sanction normal increment in respect of the government servant on production of 'Green Card' and other documents, if any, to the satisfaction of the sanctioning authority.

All the above specifications were made on 4.6.1985 vide Memo No. 22985 (350) of the Finance Department and forwarded to all the departments of the government. Further the government has specified the incentives for the 'Green Card' holders having one and two children and also for the lower category of servants. These are as follows:

(i) The Government Servants who are in possession of 'Green Cards' with 'one child' will be entitled to incentive allowance equal to twice the amount of their annual increment.

(ii) The government servants who are in possession of 'Green Cards' with two children will be entitled to incentive allowance equal to the amount of one annual increment.

(iii) Class-IV Government servants who are in possession of 'Green Cards' with one or two children will be entitled to incentive allowance equal to twice the amount of their annual increment (Memo No. F. WIG-16.91-11852/Hdt. 21/3/92).

Other Facilities

Apart from the above provisions, government has also made an attractive provision, like provision of instant financial assistance to the persons who undergo sterilization and also to those who adopt intra uterine contraception devices for controlling their family size. But the rate of instant financial assistance to the adopters is not uniform for the male and female acceptors.

However, the assistance is provided from the central as well as state governments on different heads. The important heads on which it is provided are: incentive allowance for acceptors, medicines and free dressing, diet for patient, transport of the patient after operation, payment to motivators and miscellaneous purposes, like: payment to the doctors and camp helpers. The detailed break-up of financial assistance provided is mentioned in Table 7.1 for the cases relating to male sterilization and 7.2 for the female sterilization.

Table No. 7.1 indicates that for one case of male sterilization there is an amount of Rs. 250.00 of which Rs. 180.00 is provided by the central government and the rest Rs. 70.00 is borne by the state government. And of the total amount, Rs. 120.00 (52.00%) is meant for the acceptor, which is given to him/her. The amount is budgeted as follows: Rs. 40.00 (16.00%) for purchase of medicines and dressing purpose, Rs. 10.00 (4.00%) is meant for the diet of the patient, Rs. 30.00 (12.00%) is meant for the transport purpose, and Rs. 40.00 (16.00%) is meant for miscellaneous purposes that include Rs. 10.00 (4.00%) for the doctor, Rs. 11.00 (4.4%) for the motivator, i.e. he who persuades the person for adopting this method of family planning, Rs. 3.00 (1.2%) for the staff nurse, Rs. 1.00 (0.40%) each for the attendant, sweeper and driver. Rupees 13.00 (5.20%) is meant for expenditure on community award group incentive ex-gratia payment for post operation complications treatment and for providing recanalisation, POL repair of vehicles, purchase of equipment and stores facility etc.

In respect of female sterilization relevant data have been provided in Table 7.2. The unit cost per one female sterilization is Rs. 259.00 of which Rs. 200.00 is provided by the central government and the rest Rs. 59.00 is borne by the state government. Of this total amount, Rs. 100.00 (38.61%) is paid to the acceptors, Rs. 60.00 (23.17%) is spent on medicine and dressing, Rs. 30.00 (11.58%) is paid to the patient to meet her diet expenses. An equal amount of money is meant for transport expenses of the patient. The rest amount of Rs. 40.00 (15.44%) is utilized towards miscellaneous purposes.

Apart from this, the central government also provides Rs. 16.00 towards for purchase of medicines and dress materials for IUD insertion per case.

Level of Awareness of Eligible Couples on Government Schemes and Facilities

In the earlier sections of this chapter we have noted that the government has a number of schemes and facilities for the eligible couples who adopt permanent method of family planning. But the awareness level among the public about the schemes and government facilities is very poor as sufficient campaign has not been made about such schemes and facilities.

If one looks at the data available in Table No. 7.3, it is observed that irrespective of communities, of the total 400 sample, only 21.5 per cent say that they know about the Green Card scheme, and the rest 78.5 per cent say that they do not know about this. However, of the total 200 male and 200 female spouses, more (26.5%) men than women (16.5) know about this. Further a cursory look at the data available in the same table shows that among all the four communities, more male spouses than the female ones are aware of the facilities available under this scheme. However, very few people know about particular schemes/facilities of the government. However, most of the male and female spouses know about the instant monetary assistance that is being paid at the spot during sterilization. But awareness on other facilities is very low. More number of couples know about this as because, this assistance is immediately given to the operated persons on the spot at the camp site and the news is spread in the community through lip service. On the contrary, there is not a single person in any of the four communities, who is aware about the provision of reservation of houses for the green care holders. But there are only 2 or 11.11 per cent Brahman male spouses who say that they are aware about the provision of land for landless couples who possess green card. Similarly there is one Brahman male and one female spouse who are aware about the provision of housing loan. Financial incentive, such as the personal pay for the government servants is an important provision but is known by only one Brahman woman as against 6 Brahman and 3 Chasa male spouses and there is only one Brahman (male) who are aware about the provision of reservation of seats for children of the parents having green card. On the other hand, there is not a single person in any of the four communities who knows about the lottery system. This is because, lottery is drawn occasionally and not propagated among the public frequently. However, data available in this table show that comparatively more number of Brahman male and female spouses know about the provision of green card facility and this is because of their higher educational background and higher awareness level than others.

Table—7.1: Amount of financial assistance for sterilization of male spouses

Sl. No.	*Items*	*Central share (in Rs.)*	*State share (in Rs.)*	*Total*
(1)	*(2)*	*(3)*	*(4)*	*(5)*
1	Amount for acceptor	100.00 (55.55)	30.00 (42.86)	130.00 (52.00)
2	Drugs and dressing	25.00 (13.89)	15.00 (21.43)	40.00 (16.00)
3	Diet of patient	10.00 (5.56)	–	10.00 (4.2)
4	Transport of the patient	9.00 (5.00)	21.00 (30.00)	30.00 (12.00)
5	Misc. purpose fund	36.00 (20.00)	4.00 (5.71)	40.00 (16.00)
(i)	Payment of doctor	10.00 (5.56)	–	10.00 (4.00)
(ii)	Payment to motivator	7.00 (3.89)	4.00 (5.71)	11.00 (4.4)
A	Staff nurse (nursing assistance)	3.00 (1.67)	–	3.00 (1.2)
B	Attendant	1.00 (0.56)	–	1.00 (0.40)
C	Sweeper	1.00 (0.56)	–	1.00 (10.40)
D	Driver	1.00 (0.56)	–	1.00 (0.40)
(iii)	Payment to anesthesist	–	–	–

(Contd...)

(1)	(2)	(3)	(4)	(5)
(iv)	Funds for expenditure on community award group incentive ex-gratia payment for post operative complication by facility and for providing recanalisation, POL/repair of vehicles purchase of equipment and store facilities.	13.00 (7.22)	–	13.00 (5.20)
	Total	**180.00 (100.00)**	**70.00 (100.00)**	**25.00 (100.00)**

Source: Dept. of Family Welfare, Govt. of Orissa.

Note: Figures in brackets represent percentage.

Table—7.2: Amount of financial assistance for sterilization of female spouses

Sl. No.	*Items*	*Central share (in Rs.)*	*State share (in Rs.)*	*Total (in Rs.)*
(1)	*(2)*	*(3)*	*(4)*	*(5)*
1	Amount for acceptor	75.00 (37.50)	25.00 (42.37)	100.00 (38.61)
2	Drugs and dressing	60.00 (30.0)	–	60.00 (23.17)
3	Diet of patient	20.00 (10.00)	10.00 (16.95)	30.00 (11.58)
4	Transport of the patient	10.00 (5.00)	20.00 (33.90)	30.00 (11.58)
5	Misc. purpose fund	–	–	40.00 (15.44)
(i)	Payment to doctor	8.00 (4.00)	–	8.00 (3.09)
(ii)	Payment to motivator	6.00 (3.00)	4.00 (6.78)	10.00 (3.86)
(iii)	Payment to camp helper	6.00 (3.00)	–	6.00 (2.32)

(Contd...)

(1)	(2)	(3)	(4)	(5)
A	Staff nurse (nursing assistance)	3.00 (1.50)	–	3.00 (1.16)
B	Attendant	1.00 (0.5)	–	1.00 (0.39)
C	Sweeper	1.00 (0.5)	–	1.00 (0.39)
D	Driver	1.00 (0.5)	–	1.00 (0.39)
IV	Payment to anesthesist	2.00 (1.00)	–	2.00 (0.77)
V	Funds for expenditure on community award group incentive ex-gratia payment for post operative complication by facility and for providing recanalisation, POL/repair of vehicles purchase of equipment and store facilities.	13.00 (6.50)	–	13.00 (5.02)
	Total	**200.00 (100.00)**	**59.00 (100.00)**	**259.00 (100.00)**

Source: Dept. of Family Welfare, Govt. of Orissa.

Note: Figures in brackets represent percentage.

Table—7.3: Level of awareness of couples on green card

Variables	*Brahman*		*Chasa*		*Bauri*		*Santal*		*Total*		*G. Total*
	W N = 50	H N = 50	W N = 50	H N = 50	W N = 50	H N = 50	W N = 50	H N = 50	W N = 200	H N = 200	N = 400
(1)	(2)	(3)	(4)	(5)	(6)	(7)	(8)	(9)	(10)	(11)	(12)
Yes	6 (12.00)	18 (36.00)	8 (16.00)	9 (18.00)	13 (26.00)	17 (34.00)	6 (12.00)	9 (18.00)	33 (16.5)	53 (26.5)	86 (21.5)
No	44 (88.00)	32 (64.00)	42 (84.00)	41 (82.00)	37 (74.00)	33 (66.00)	44 (88.00)	41 (82.00)	167 (83.5)	147 (73.5)	314 (78.5)

Note: (*i*) Figures in brackets represent percentage.

(*ii*) N is 50 for wife and also for husband of each caste.

Table—7.4: Level of awareness of couples on different sectoral schemes of green card

Variable	*Brahman*		*Chasa*		*Bauri*		*Santal*		*Total*		*G. Total*
	W *N = 6*	*H* *N = 18*	*W* *N = 8*	*H* *N = 9*	*W* *N = 13*	*H* *N = 17*	*W* *N = 6*	*H* *N = 9*	*W* *N = 33*	*H* *N = 53*	*N = 86*
(1)	*(2)*	*(3)*	*(4)*	*(5)*	*(6)*	*(7)*	*(8)*	*(9)*	*(10)*	*(11)*	*(12)*
Reservation of houses	–	–	–	–	–	–	–	–	–	–	–
Provision of land for landless	–	2 (11.11)	–	–	–	–	–	–	–	2 (3.77)	2 (2.33)
Provision of housing loan	1 (16.62)	1 (5.56)	–	–	–	–	–	–	1 (3.03)	1 (1.89)	2 (2.33)
Financial incentive to Govt. servants	1 (16.62)	6 (33.33)	–	3 (33.33)	–	–	–	–	1 (3.03)	9 (16.98)	10 (11.63)
Lottery scheme	–	–	–	–	–	–	–	–	–	–	–
Reservation of seats for children	–	1 (5.56)	–	1 (11.11)	–	–	–	–	–	2 (3.77)	2 (2.33)
Instant monetary assistance	2 (33.33)	11 (61.11)	3 (3.75)	9 (100.00)	13 (100.00)	12 (70.59)	6 (100.00)	8 (85.8[illegible])	24 (72.73)	40 (75.4)	64 (74.42)

Note: Figures in brackets represent percentage.

CHAPTER–VIII

Critical Review on Government Facilities and Suggestions

In the previous chapter, we have discussed about the schemes and facilities available for the family planning adopters, particularly the persons who undergo sterilization and those who use terminal methods for avoiding unwanted pregnancies and hence to have a desirable family size according to one's own choice and need. However, in this regard the policies, plans and programmes for encouraging the couples for adopting family planning methods, seem to be very erroneous which must be rectified and a logical and feasible action plan be implemented for achieving the goal by bringing down the decennial population growth rate. Some important suggestions have been given below for more successful operation of family planning programmes in India.

(i) India is a very vast and diverse country having more than 100 crore of population belonging to hundreds of races, cultures, communities, religions and ethnicities, whose ideology and moral values differ from one another because of various diversities and local situations. Most of them live in rural areas and are tradition-bound. They consider the children as the gift of God and think that the number of children a couple gets is absolutely dependent upon the will of the God and hence one must not go against this

natural process. If at all a person makes any artificial attempt to reduce his/her family size, he/she may go against the divine will and as a result he/she may face a number of mishaps. Therefore, the first and foremost duty of the government as well as non-government agencies should be focussed on motivation of these communities about the need for reducing the family size. This programme must be initiated immediately through various electronic media, like, television, film, radio etc. and other non-electronic media, like newspapers, posters, magazines, etc. Apart from all these, attempt should be made to focus the importance of family planning through local folk shows, drama, theatre, rallies, etc. It must be compulsory for all the media including film halls for spreading the message of family planning, through each and every film shows, otherwise the defaulters be deprived of Government advertisements and there should be heavy cash fine. Further, it would be better if government plans to propagate the family planning message through all the programmes, and episodes that are telecast in television. Similarly, it should be mandatory for all the local, regional and national newspapers to publish massages on family planning daily. This would certainly create a significant impact on the public. Apart from all these the campaign should also be made by use of audio systems, like mike sets.

(ii) In our country, family planning measures are suggestive. In this context we may refer to the second point of the Government Resolution, No. Fw-IG-3/81 (pt), 34707/H.d 19.10.83, in which it is mentioned that until family welfare becomes a truly popular and participatory programme, some incentives have to be offered as "motivational measures". This sentence signifies that Government is very liberal and suggests that one should adopt family planning method, and if one does so, he/she would get some incentives or

reward. But now, we have already crossed 100 crore mark in our population size and there is now a very heavy pressure on the existing natural resources. This would bring to an end of the whole human civilization if no rigid and feasible action is immediately taken up to restrict the amazing population growth. Therefore, our action plans relating to family planning must be compulsive instead of being suggestive for both the Government as well as non-government servants. It should also be applicable to the public and there must not be any provision of cash payment or other incentives for the family planning adaptors. The punishment system for the service holders in public and private sectors should tentatively be as follows:

(a) A government employee who procreates more than two children, should be denied of promotion facility.

(b) His/her annual increment should be stopped.

(c) No loan facility from his/her office or any financial institution for any purpose be available to him/her.

These rules be enforced for all Indian people irrespective of castes, religions, communities etc. At the initial stage there may be protest against the government from various castes or communities, but in due course of time the initiative would be fruitful. Apart from these measures the following two initiatives should be carried out.

(i) Earlier we have discussed about the monetary assistance which is given to the men and women who undergo sterilization. An amount of Rs. 250/- as against Rs. 259/- is earmarked for male and female sterilization respectively. Of the total amount specified for male sterilization, only Rs. 130/- which is 52 per cent, of the amount is given to the acceptor and of the total amount specified for female sterilization only Rs. 100/- which is merely 38.61 per cent of the

amount is given to the female acceptor of sterilization method and the rest amount is spent for other purposes, like dressing, diet of the patient, transport of the patient, payment to doctor, staff nurse, camp helpers, attendants, sweepers, drivers etc. But when these persons, like doctors, staff nurse, etc. are government servants, and as such, their duty is to serve the public, then why such a provision has been made? They are getting their salary for their services. Therefore, there is no justification for paying extra incentive in cash while they do their official job either at family planning centre or at the camp sites. This must immediately be withdrawn and the incentives that they are getting be given to the acceptors who adopt the permanent family planning measures.

(ii) The amount of incentives which is earmarked for the acceptors, is very meagre. It must be enhanced and must be made more lucrative to the public by which they would be motivated and interested to adopt family planning measures.

CHAPTER—IX

SUMMARY AND CONCLUSION

Indian population is growing very fast and it has become a matter of great concern for all of us as heavy pressure is steadily mounting on the existing natural resources. However, the reasons of high population growth in our country are many and each cause is multidimensional and dependent on other factors. Moreover, the factors responsible for high growth rate of population may be attributed to various problems which relate to folk beliefs, traditional culture, religion, lack of education, level of awareness, economy, role of media, physical and social environment etc. Therefore, in order to reduce population growth, government has introduced various schemes and facilities for the people for adopting family welfare measures.

Keeping, the above fact in mind, an attempt has been made to find out different dimensions of family welfare measures among four communities residing in fringe villages of the capital city of Bhubaneswar. These are: the Brahman from upper caste Hindu social order, Chasa, from middle caste Hindu social order and Bauri, a Scheduled Caste community and Santal, a Scheduled Tribe community who are outside the pale of Hindu social order, or traditional *Varna* organisation. Thus, the study is meant to provide a cross-cultural picture on the population problem and family welfare measures at the grassroots level.

The universe of the study constitutes a total number of 200 eligible couples; 50 each from the above communities living in and around Bhubaneswar city, the state capital of Orissa.

The broad aims and objectives of the study and nine-fold in nature. These are as follows:

(i) to find out the opinion on marriage and attainment of parenthood among the target populations;

(ii) to find out the opinion on sex preference in birth and importance of son vis-à-vis daughter in the family;

(iii) to find out the attitude of men and women towards family planning and adoption of birth control measures;

(iv) to find out adoption of birth control measures among the eligible couples;

(v) to find out the sources of information and knowledge on family planning and birth control measures;

(vi) to find out the reasons for adoption and non-adoption of birth control measures;

(vii) to find out the post-operation complications among the sterilized couples, if any;

(viii) to find out the awareness level of people on government schemes/facilities available on adoption of family planning; and

(ix) to provide a recipe for better implementation and success of family planning programmes.

The major findings of the study are as follows:

(a) all the four communities studied are patriarchal, patriolocal, patrilineal, and patronymic in nature and hence in these communities the socio-cultural and economic importance of men is more than the women. Therefore, people desire to have boy children.

(b) all male and female spouses of each community are of the opinion that one should get married and procreate children.

(c) so far as the number of children one should get is concerned, 70 per cent of Santal followed by 48 per

cent of Brahman and 28 per cent of Bauri say that one should have two children but most of the Chasa (38%) say that one should have a maximum of three children. And most of them want that they should have boy children. This is so because of the ongoing cultural and religious set practices where the social, ritual and economic role and duties of male children are of greater importance than the female children. Thus the attitude and age-old mindset towards a boy child does not permit a couple to plan or limit its family, rather it comples the couple to go on procreating children until at least one boy child is born to them.

(d) Out of the total sample of 50 female spouses of each community as many as 86 per cent of Brahman as against 74 per cent of Chasa, 56 per cent of Bauri and only 14 per cent of Santal are of the opinion that a couple should limit its family size, and the rest go against this opinion and put forth various reasons to justify their opinion. Irrespective of any community, they say that it is against the will of God. A total number of 67 spouses, accounting for 51.54 per cent, say that more income is feasible if one has more number of sons. And the other reasons are: sharing of problems of family (9.23%), security and protection of family (6.92%), it is anti-religious (5.38%) and 3.8 per cent said that they are afraid of bad or harmful physical consequences of family planning.

(e) Currently a total number of 20 Brahman (40%) as against 16 Chasa (32%), 21 Bauri (42%) and 8 Santal (16%) couples are adopting modern family planning measures and the rest do not adopt. Of the total 20 Brahman, 16 Chasa, 21 Bauri and 8 Santal couples who are currently adopting family planning measures, 11 or 55 per cent of Brahman, 14 or 87.5 per cent of Chasa, 17 or 80.95 per cent of Bauri and 7 or 87.50 per cent of Santal have adopted sterilization method of family planning.

(f) Of the total sterilization cases in each community, most of them are women. It is 10 or 90.91 per cent for Brahman, 11 or 78.57 per cent of Chasa, 17 or 100 per cent for Bauri and 6 or 85.91 per cent for Santal. The rest are male sterilization.

(g) Irrespective of any community, out of the total of 65 couples adopting family planning devices, 44 or 67.69 per cent have gone in for tubectomy as against 5 or 7.69 of per cent vasectomy cases. There are only 5 couples, accounting for 7.69 per cent, who are using copper-T or other Intra-Uterine Devices (IUDs). Use of oral pills is limited to only 7 or 10.77 per cent of couples and there are only 4 or 6.15 per cent of couples using condom.

(h) Out of the total female spouses who have been sterilized, 4 or 40 per cent of Brahman, 6 or 54.55 per cent of Chasa, 13 or 76.47 per cent of Bauri and 6 or 100 per cent of Santal have adopted this method voluntarily and the rest have been persuaded to do so.

(i) So far as the reasons for female sterilization are concerned, irrespective of any community, out of the total of 44 tubectomy cases, 34 or 77.77 per cent of women say that they have adopted this with a view not to trouble their husbands, who are the main bread-winners of their families. If they suffer then that would affect the economy of their households. A total number of 38 male spouses of the total sterilized female spouses are of this opinion.

(j) As regards the knowledge of all couples (both adopters and non-adopters) on family planning methods, it is found that every male and female spouse of the study communities has knowledge on at least one modern family planning measures. Whereas all the male and female spouses of each community have knowledge on both male as well as female sterilization measures.

(*k*) So far as the source of information and knowledge on the methods of family planning among the adopting couples is concerned, for the men, these are: ANM/ doctor (44.62%), radio (44.62%), television (43.08%), friends (36.46%), neighbours (21.44%), relatives other than own spouse (10.77%), PHCs/hospitals (4.62%), newspapers/magazines (3.08%) and posters (1.5%), and for female spouses, these are: television (81.54%), friends (69.23%), radio (41.54%), newspapers/ magazines (29.62%), ANM/doctor (27.69%), PHC/ hospital (13.85%), relatives other than own spouse (10.77%), posters (3.08%), and own spouse (1.54%).

(*l*) Of the total females sterilized, 5 (50%) Brahman, 2 (18.18%) Chasa, 7 (41.18%) Bauri, and 4 (66.67%) Santal, claim that they did not suffer from any problem after they were sterilized. The rest, however, suffered from one problem or other.

(*m*) The problem from which they suffered are: headache (65.38%), abdominal pain (46.15%), waist pain (19.23%), joint pain (11.54%) dizziness (7.69%), gastritis (3.85%) and delay in healing of a wound (3.85%).

(*n*) Of the total 5 male spouses who have been sterilized, 2 (40%) are suffering from post-operation problem and the rest are fine. Both these persons are suffering from dizziness and one of them is also suffering from abdominal pain.

(*o*) Government has various schemes/facilities for couples who follow two-children norm. Ready cash is paid to the couples for undergoing sterilization at the time of operation and there is a provision of cash assistance for diet of such persons. Apart from these, there is a green card scheme for the couples who have one or two children and have been sterilized. The schemes include reservation of houses on allotment from Government Housing Scheme, provision of land for landless couples, provision of housing loan, sanction of extra increment in personal salary for the government employees, reservation of the seats for the children of green-card holders in different educational institutions and jobs etc. But in spite of all these, the levels of awareness of people is very low about the family planning schemes/facilities of the government.

References And Bibliography

Acharya, R and S. Sureender, 1996, "Inter-spouse Communication, Contraceptive Use and Family Size: Relationship Examined in Bihar and Tamil Nadu", *The Journal of Family Welfare*, Vol. 42, (4): 5-11.

Agarwala, S.N., 1962, *Age at Marriage in India*. Bombay: Kitab Mahal Pvt. Ltd.

——, 1964, "Social and Cultural Factors Affecting in India", *Population Review*, 8: 73–78.

——, 1967, *India's Population Problem*, New Delhi: Tata McGraw Hill Pub. Co.

Ahuja, Ram, 1992, *Rights of Women—A Feministic Perspective*, New Delhi: Rawat.

Aiyer, Swaminathan and S. Anklesaria, 1996, "The Family is an Insurance Mechanism", *The Times of India*, New Delhi, December 31.

Altekar, A.S., 1959, *The Position of Women in Hindu Civilization*. Delhi: Motilal Banarasi Dass Publishers.

Andorka, Rudolf, 1982, *Determinants of Fertility in Advanced Societies*. London: Methuen and Co. Ltd.

Arnold, Fred et al., 1975, *The Value of Children: A Cross-National Study*. Honolulu: East West Population Institute.

Arora, G. 1983, "Socio-Economic Determinants of Fertility", *Journal of Family Welfare*, XXIX (3): 3–9.

Arora, Gomati, 1990, *Social Structure and Fertility*, New Delhi: National Books Organisation.

Asif, Rashmi et al., 1994, "Contraceptive Behaviour in Women Carrying an Unwanted Pregnancy", *The Journal of Family Welfare*, Vol. 40, (2): 26-30.

Balaiah, D, 2001, "Fertility Attitudes and Family Planning Practices of Men in a Rural Community of Maharashtra", *The Journal of Family Welfare*, Vol. 47, (1): 56–67.

Bebarta, P.C., 1960, *A Study of Differential Fertility in Certain Villages of Coastal Orissa*. Bombay: Demographic Training and Research Institute (Mimeo).

——, 1964, "Family Structure and Fertility", *Proceedings of The Indian Science Congress Association*. Part III, 51st and 52nd Session, Anthropology Section, Calcutta.

Behura, N.K, and R.P. Mohanty, 1999, *Status and Empowerment of the Girl Child and the Woman in the Contemporary Societies—A Cross-Cultural Study in Orissa*. Bhubaneswar: NKC Centre for Development Studies (Project Report).

Benerji, D., 1996, *Family Measurement in India*, New Delhi: Sage.

Bharat, Shalini (ed), 1971, *Family Planning in India*. New Delhi: People's Pub. House.

Bhat, T.N., 1997, "Social Change and Family Planning: A Case Study of Backward Classes", *The Journal of Family Welfare*, Vol. 43, (4): 25-45.

Bhatiya, J.C., 1967, "Attitudinal Study of Rural Males in Punjab Village", *Family Planning News*, 8: 7-9.

Bhuyan, K.C., 1996, "Differential Fertility Among Adopter and Non-Adopter Couples of Differing Social Status and Mobility Pattern in Rural Bangladesh—A Case Study", *The Journal of Family Welfare*, Vol. 42, (3): 46-50.

Cain, M, 1981, "Risk and Insurance: Perspective on Fertility and Agrarian Change in India and Bangladesh", *Population and Development Review*, 7: 435-74.

Caldwell, John C., 1983, "Direct Economic Costs and Benefits of Children", in Rodolf, a and others (eds), *Determinants of Fertility in Developing Countries*, New York: Academic Press.

Chakrabartty, K, 2002, *Family in India*, Jaipur: Rawat.

Cherian, V.I., 1994, "Maternal and Paternal Aspirations and Academic Achievement of Xhosa Children from Broken and Intact Families", *The Journal of Family Welfare*, Vol. 40, No. 3: 26-31.

Choudhury, Rafiqul Hyder, 1982, *Social Aspects of Fertility*. New Delhi: Vikas.

Coombs, L.C., 1978, "Husband—Wife Agreement About Reproductive Goals". *Demography*, 15: 57-73.

Das, M.S. and P.D. Bardis, 1979, *The Family in Asia*. London: George Allen and Unwin.

Deka, N.K, 1996, "Between Group Variations in Desire for Future Births: A Demographic Study", *The Journal of Family Welfare*, Vol. 42, (3): 32-36.

Desai, A.R., 1980, *Urban Family and Family Planning in India*. Bombay: Popular Prakashan.

Driver, E.D., 1960, "Fertility Differentials among Economic Strata in Central India", *Eugenics Quarterly*, 7 (June): 77-85.

Dubey, S.M. et al, 1980, *Family Marriage and Social Change in Indian Fringe*. New Delhi: Cosmo.

Dutta, Sudipt, 1997, *Family Business in India*. Delhi: Sage.

GoI, 1991, *Provisional Population Tables*, Paper 2 of 1991, Series I. New Delhi: Census of India.

——, 1991, *Provisional Population Tables*, Series 19, Orissa, Paper I of 1991. New Delhi: Census of India.

——, 1991, *General Population Tables*, Series 19, Orissa, Part-IIA, New Delhi: Census of India.

——, 1991, *General Population Tables* A to A_3, Part II A(i). New Delhi: Census of India.

——, 1991, *Towards a Better Future*, New Delhi: Directorate of Advertising and Visual Publicity, Ministry of Information and Broadcasting.

——, 1996, *Statistical Outline of India*, 1995-96, Bombay: Tata Services Ltd. for Dept. of Economics and Statistics.

——, 1999, *Selected Socio-Economic Statistics, India*. New Delhi: Central Statistical Organisation, Ministry of Statistics and Programme Implementation.

——, 2000, *National Population Policy—2000*, New Delhi: Dept. of Health and Family Welfare.

GoO, 1979, *Statistical Abstract*, Bhubaneswar: Directorate of Economics and Statistics.

——, 1981, *Statistical Abstract*. Bhubaneswar: Directorate of Economics and Statistics.

——, 1983, *A Booklet on Green Card Scheme*. Bhubaneswar: Dept. of Health and Family Welfare.

——, 1990, *Green Card*. Bhubaneswar: Dept. of Health and Family Welfare.

——, 1991, *Statistical Abstract*. Bhubaneswar: Directorate of Economics and Statistics.

——, 1996, *Statistical Abstract*. Bhubaneswar: Directorate of Economics and Statistics.

——, 1996, *Memo No. 16303/FW/BTU/5.92*. Bhubaneswar, dt. 3.7.96; Dept. of Health and Family Welfare.

——, 2000, *A Booklet on Greet Card Scheme*. Bhubaneswar: Dept. of Health and Family Welfare.

Goode, J.W., 1987, *The Family*. New Delhi: Prentice Hall of India Pvt. Ltd.

Gurumurthy, G., 1990, *Culture and Fertility Behaviour of Yanadis*. Bombay: Himalaya Pub. House.

Guruswamy, M. and S. Sureender, 1987, "Conventional Contraceptives: Towards a Selective Policy of Free Institution in India", *Journal of Family Welfare*, Vol. 43 (4): 17-21.

Gould, H.K., 1969, "Sex Contraception in Sherpur: Family Planning in North Indian Village", *EPW*, IV (19): 1887-1892.

Hoffman, Lois and H.L. Hoffman, 1973, "The Value of Children to Parents", James T. Fawcetted. *Psychological Perspectives on Population*, New York: Basic Books.

Joesting, J, and R. Joesting, 1973, "Birth Order and Desired Family Size", *Journal of Individual Psychology*, 29: 3-9.

Kale, B.D., 1966, "Family Planning Knowledge and Attitudes in High Population Growth Rate Area", *Journal of Institute of Economic Research*, 1: 5-20.

Kanitkar, S.D., 1996, "Gender Discrimination in the Family: Views and Experience of Teenage Girls", *The Journal of Family Welfare*, Vol. 42, (4): 32-38.

Kolenda, Pauline, 1968, "Religion, Caste and Family: Co-operative Study of the Indian Joint Family", in M. Singh and B. Cohn (eds) *Structure and Change in Indian Society*, Chicago: Aldine Pub. Co.

Kumar, A.K., 1994, "Orissa's Population Growth and, Fertility Change", *The Journal of Family Welfare*, Vol. 40, (1): 44-48.

Lodha, Neeta and Kumawat, Lalit, 2002, "Status of Tribal Women and Fertility", *Madhya Pradesh Journal of Social Sciences*, Vol. 7, (1): 74-84.

Mahadevan, K., 1979, *Sociology of Fertility: Determinants of Fertility Differences in South India*. Delhi: Sterling.

Mahadevan, K., 1989, *Fertility Policies of Asian Countries (ed)*. New Delhi: Sage.

Minkler, M., 1970, "Fertility and Female Labour Force Participation in India: A Survey of Working in Old Delhi Area", *Journal of Family Welfare*. 17 (1): 31-43.

Mukherjee, R., 1976, *Family and Family Planning in India*, New Delhi: Orient Longman.

Mukherji, S., 1998, "Family Planning and Target Setting", *The Journal of Family Welfare*, Vol. 44, (2): 25-27.

Nag, Moni, 1972, "Sex, Culture and Human Fertility", *Current Anthropologists*. 13 (2): 231-40.

——, 1968, *Factors Affecting Human Fertility in Non-Industrial Societies—A Cross Cultural Study*, Yale University Publications in Anthropology New Haven, No. 66 Reprinted in 1968 (1962).

Nanda, S and S. Sureender, 1997, "Female Work Status and its Relationship with Fertility and Child Loss in Orissa", *Journal of Family Welfare*, 43 (3): 34-37.

Ojha, A., 1998, "The Effect of Sex Preference on Fertility in Selected States of India", *The Journal of Family Welfare*, Vol. 44 (1): 42-48.

Pakrasi, Kaunti and M. Chittranjan, 1967, "The Relationship between Family Type and Fertility", *Millsank Memorial Fund*. 45: 451-60.

Pandey, G.D. and R.S. Tiwari, 2001, "Socio-Cultural Reproductive Health Practices of Primitive Tribes of Madhya Pradesh: Some Observations", *The Journal of Family Welfare*, Vol. 47 (2): 27-33.

PRC and IIPS, 1993, *National Family Health Survey*. Bhubaneswar: Population Research Centre (Utkal University) and International Institute for Population Science (Bombay).

Patel, T., 1994, *Fertility Behaviour—Population and Society in a Rajasthan Village*. Bombay: Oxford University Press.

Pathak, K.B. and A. Panday, 1994, *Bio-social Aspects of Human Fertility—Models and Applications*. Delhi: B.R. Publishing Corporation.

Puri, Nina, 1998, "The Girl Child in India", *The Journal of Family Welfare*, Vol. 44 (3): 1-8.

Raina, B.L., 1990, *Planning Family in India—Pre-vedic Times to Early 1950*, New Delhi: Commonwealth Publishers.

Rainwater, Lee, 1965, *Family Design: Marital Sexuality, Family Size and Contraception*. Chicago: Aldine Pub. Co.

Rajeswari, N.V. and J.B. Hasalkar, 1996, "IUD Retention in Shimoger District of Karnataka", *The Journal of Family Welfare*, Vol. 42 (1): 44-50.

Ramu, G.N., 1987, "Indian Husbands: Their Role Perception and Performance in Single and Dual Earner Families", *Journal of Marriage and the Family*. 49-903-15.

——, 1988, *Family Structure and Fertility Emerging Patterns in an Indian City*. New Delhi: Sage.

Rao, N.B., 1976, *Family Planning in India*. New Delhi: Vikas.

Rao, A.V. Subba, 1968, "Vasectomy in Rural Areas of Andhra Pradesh", *Family Planning News*, 9 (4): 14-19.

Rao, P.H. 1996, "The Family Planning Programme and Contraceptive Use in India: A Marketing Perspective", *The Journal of Family Welfare*, Vol. 42 (2): 14-20.

Reddy, M. and K. Mahadevan, 1986, "Values Attached to Male and Female Children", *Social Change*, 16 (1): 45-48.

Reddy, M.M.K., 1996, *Fertility and Family Planning Behaviour in Indian Society (ed)*, New Delhi: Kanishka Publishers and Distributors.

Reddy, M.M.K, 1997, *Two-Child Family Norms in Rural India—Problems and Prospects*. New Delhi: Kaniska Publishers and Distributors.

Reddy, Muni Krishna, 1985, "Sex Combination of Living Children and Adoption of Sterilization—A Rural Study in Andhra Pradesh", *Journal of Family Welfare*, XXX1 (4): 61-68.

Reddy, P.H., 1978, "Family Structure and Fertility", *Social Change*, 8 (1): 24-32.

Rele, J.R, 1962, "Some Aspect of Family and Fertility in India, *Population Studies*, 15 (3): 267-278.

Repetto, Robert, 1972, "Son Preferences and Fertility Behaviour in Developing Countries", *Studies in Family Planning*, 3 (4): 70.

Ridkar, R.G. 1969, "Desired Family Size and The Efficacy of Current Family Planning Programmes", *Population Studies*, 23: 279-284.

Rosenzweig, R. Marn, 1982, "Educational Subsidy, Agricultural Development and Fertility Change", *The Quarterly Journal of Economics*, XCVII (1): 67-88.

Sarkar, N.N., 1996, "Acceptability and Efficacy of the Female Condom: A New Barrier Method", *The Journal of Family Welfare*, Vol. 42 (2): 41-48.

Saxena, G.B., 1965, "Differential Fertility in Rural Hindu Community: A Sample Survey of Rural Uttar Pradesh", *Eugenic Quarterly*, 12.

Sekhar, S.P. and C.P. Nagi Reddy, 1994, "Regional Variations in Contraceptive Choice in Andhra Pradesh", *The Journal of Family Welfare*, Vol. 40 (2): 51-60.

Sen, Narayan, 2001, "Differences in Family Planning Status Between the Middle Class and Poor in Calcutta: The Reasons and Remedies—A Comparative Study", *The Journal of Family Welfare*, Vol. 47 (1): 14-27.

Shah, A.M., 1998, *The Family in India—Critical Essays*. New Delhi: Orient Longman.

Shariff, Abusaleh, 1989, *Fertility Transition in Rural South India*. New Delhi: Gian.

Sinha, Amarjeet and Arvinder Kaur, 1997, "Oral Contraceptive Use in a Rural Area in Haryana", *The Journal of Family Welfare*, 43 (4): 64-68.

Sinha, J.N., 1957, "Differential Fertility and Fertility Limitations in an Urban Community of Uttar Pradesh", *Population Studies*, 11 (2): 157-69.

Srinivas, M.N. and E.A. Ramaswamy, 1977, *Cultural and Human Fertility*, New Delhi: Oxford University Press.

Sinha, R.K. and Kanitkar, T., 1994, "Acceptance of Family Planning and Linkages with Development Variables", *The Journal of Family Welfare*, Vol. 40, (2): 14-17.

Stokes, Sharon and N.E. Johnson, 1977, Birth Order, Size of Family of Orientation and Desired Family Size, *Journal of Individual Psychology*, 33: 32-42.

The Samaj, 2000, *Jhio Janma Hebaru Nirjyatana* (24.7.2000).

——, 2000, *Jhio Janma Karibaru Strira naka katila Swami* (16.12.2000).

Uberoi, Patricia, 1993, "Problems with Patriarchy: Conceptual Issues in anthropology and Feminism", *Sociological Bulletin,* 44 (2): 195-222.

Verma, R.K. and Baburanjan, P.K, 1994, "Determinants of Contraceptive Choice in India", *The Journal of Family Welfare,* Vol. 40 (3): 1-8.

Verma, K.K., 1992, *Health Care and Family Welfare.* New Delhi: Mittal.

Visaria, Pravin, 1989, *Determinants of Couple Protection Rates in India: A District Level Survey,* Working Paper No. 25, Ahmedabad: Gujarat, Institute of Development Research.

Visaria, Pravin, Leela Visaria and Anrudh Jain, 1995, *Contraceptive Use and Fertility in India—A Case of Gujarat.* New Delhi: Sage.

Wolanski, N. and Barry Bogin, 1996, *The Family as an Environment for Human Development.* Delhi: Kamla—Raj Enterprises.

World Bank, 1996, *Improving Women's Health in India.* Washington D.C.: The World Bank.

Yadav, S.S. and Badari, V.S. 1997, "Age at Effective Marriage and Fertility: An Analysis of Data for North Kanara, *Journal of Family Welfare,* 43 (3): 61-66.

Young, C.M., 1974, Numbers of Children Planned. Expected and Preferred by Women in Melbourne, *Journal of Biosocial Science,* 6: 295-304.

Index